ENDURANCE

A Widow's Insight into Workplace Tragedy

JACQUELINE QUINLIVAN

First Published in Australia in 2026
By Morpheus Publishing
Geelong Victoria 3216
www.morpheuspublishing.com.au

Paperback ISBN:	**978-1-923650-17-6**
Ebook:	**978-1-923650-18-3**
Ingram ISBN:	**978-1-923650-19-0**
Author:	**Jacqueline Quinlivan**
Editor:	**Hannah Pearce**
Cover Graphics:	**Mylan Carascal**
Typesetting:	**Oseyi Okoeguale**

A catalogue record for this book is available from the National Library of Australia.

DISCLAIMER
The information contained in this book is for general informational purposes only. The author and publisher are not offering any medical, legal or professional advice. While every effort has been made to ensure the accuracy and completeness of the information provided, the author and publisher assume no responsibility for errors or omissions or any outcomes or consequences resulting from using this book's content.

DISTRIBUTION
This book is distributed by Morpheus Publishing and is available through authorised distributors, booksellers, Morpheus Publishing website.

PUBLISHER: Morpheus Publishing
www.morpheuspublishing.com.au | hello@morpheuspublising.com.au | +61403 564 942

AUTHOR: Jacqueline Quinlivan
https://www.morpheuspublishing.com.au/authors/jacqueline-quinlivan

CONTENTS

Dedication and Acknowledgment v

Foreword by Patrizia Cassaniti vii

Introduction 1

Chapter 1: My Passion = Your Legacy 5

Chapter 2: A Teenage Romance Blossomed into Forever 13

Chapter 3: Adversity hit us hard! 23

Chapter 4: Our Amazing Wedding 35

Chapter 5: Could We Have Children? 47

Chapter 6: The Time of Our Lives 59

Chapter 7: A Preventable Workplace Incident 73

Chapter 8: Adversity Hit Again, Even Harder 87

Chapter 9: Financial Implications 101

Chapter 10: Failures Turned Into Learnings 109

Chapter 11: A Day for All Workers 115

Chapter 12: A Belly Full of Fire 121

Chapter 13: Out on My Own 131

Chapter 14: Meeting Inspirational People 141

Chapter 15: Parenting Whilst Grief Stricken 151

Book Jacqueline as a *Safety Speaker* today 163

Important Contacts 165

References 167

DEDICATION AND ACKNOWLEDGMENT

This book is dedicated first and foremost to Lyndon, my husband: Even still, after all these years, your support (albeit from heaven) is still my shining light and has kept me going.

To my amazing kids, Chris and Mia: Being your mother is by far, the best job in the world and although life threw us one hell of a curveball, you have both supported me in ways you could never possibly imagine. This is for you, to know that with family, love and support, the world is your oyster. Your dad would be exceptionally proud of the people you are growing into, just as I am.

To my parents, both my mother and my in-laws: Your unwavering support has not gone unnoticed. Words simply cannot describe my love for each of you and my eternal gratitude.

I could go on for ages listing everyone else who has given me the strength I needed to propel forward in such dark times, but this is merely an acknowledgement – You each know who you are. From the bottom of my heart, a huge thank you.

Lastly, I won't get to meet everyone who reads this book in the future, however, my gratitude needs to also go out to YOU! You read my book which in turn brings the safety messages within this book to the forefront of your minds, and that is my mission. So a very big shoutout goes to YOU for being you. Never forget, you are important and you are AMAZING.

FOREWORD
BY PATRIZIA CASSANITI

I have had the privilege of knowing Jacci for the past five years—though, like so many relationships formed in this space, ours began in the most heartbreaking of circumstances. We did not meet through joy or celebration, but through unimaginable loss. The loss of her husband, Lyndon, and the loss of my son, Christopher. Loss that no family should ever have to endure, yet far too many of us do.

After Christopher tragically died at work in 2019, my life was forever changed. I became part of an advisory group made up of families, who had lost loved ones at work, alongside workers who had been seriously injured. This group was united not just by grief, but by a fierce determination to drive change—real, lasting change at a government and systemic level. It was within this space that I met Jacci.

From the very beginning, I felt an undeniable connection to her. We had been thrust into a world we never asked to enter. There was something immediately familiar about Jacci. She carried the same fire in her heart and belly that I did. The same anger. The same pain. The same refusal to accept that our loved ones would be reduced to statistics, liabilities, or line items in a compensation claim. We both knew, deep in our bones, that Christopher and Lyndon did not die in vain—and we would spend the rest of our lives ensuring that truth was known.

Although we met through tragedy, the bond we have built in a relatively short time is profound. It is forged through shared grief, shared battles, and a shared mission. We understand each other without needing to explain the unexplainable. We have stood beside one another through the relentless exhaustion of advocacy, through moments of despair, and through the small but meaningful wins that remind us why we keep going.

Jacci's advocacy resonated deeply with me because it mirrors my own journey. Like me, she has taken the worst moment of her life and transformed it into purpose. Together, we made a choice—not an easy one—to channel our pain into action. To turn heartbreak into fuel. That fuel has become the foundation of the work we do today.

I have been an advocate and a speaker since Christopher died. I do this because I have no choice. When you lose a child at work, silence is no longer an option. I speak because Christopher cannot. I advocate because no other family should ever receive the phone call that shattered my world. Jacci has now begun to share her story too, bravely stepping into this space, following a path no one should ever have to walk—but one that is necessary if change is to occur.

This book is not just Lyndon's story. It is a legacy. Just as my work carries Christopher's name, Jacci's work carries Lyndon's. Their lives mattered. Their deaths matter. And the lessons written in these pages have the power to save lives—if people are willing to listen.

Those who choose to read this book do so not for comfort, but for awareness. For truth. For accountability. Jacci writes with a clear mission: to bring workplace safety to the forefront of every conversation, every job site, every decision made by employers, regulators, and workers themselves. Her hope—our shared hope—is that complacency ends here. That workers find the courage to say no when something is unsafe. That employers place human life above profit. And that systems finally reflect compassion rather than cruelty. Because the reality is this: when a worker dies, families like ours are treated as though we no longer matter.

We have both felt the full wrath of what it is like to lose a loved one at work and then be forced to navigate a system that re-traumatises us at every turn. A system where our loved ones are reduced to liabilities. Where civil cases and compensation processes feel less like justice and more like interrogation. Where grieving families are the ones who end up feeling as though we are on trial. It is torture.

No family should ever be put through this. Not after the devastation of knowing your loved one will never walk through the door again. Not after the unbearable finality of a life stolen simply because of a workplace incident.

The current compensation system is broken. It needs a complete revamp—one that recognises the humanity of families, not just legal frameworks and financial limits. Jacci and I hope that through our advocacy, our voices, and our influence, change will come. Not only to convince workers to stop being complacent, but to empower them to speak up. To walk away from danger. To value their lives above deadlines, pressure, or fear. And beyond that, we hope to drive further legislative and systemic reform—so families like ours are treated with dignity, compassion, and respect.

This mission does not stop at Australia's borders. Workplace death is a global issue. Workers everywhere deserve to return home safely. This book speaks not only to Australians, but to workers, families, and communities all over the world.

Jacci is, in many ways, a reflection of myself. She is relentless. She is courageous. And she will not give up until meaningful change is achieved. I admire her strength, her persistence, and her unwavering voice. We push each other forward when the road becomes too heavy. We remind one another why this work matters—on the days when grief threatens to silence us.

Losing Christopher changed me forever. As a person. As a mother. As a wife. There is no version of me untouched by that loss. And yet, in that darkness, I found purpose. I will continue to fight tooth and nail for what is right—for Christopher, for Lyndon, and for every worker, because they deserve to come home. While justice can never truly be served for our loved ones we've already lost, the future can change. Laws can be strengthened. Workplaces can be made safer. Lives can be saved.

This book is an invitation—to listen, to learn, and to act.

No one should ever go to work then not be able to come home.

No family should ever live our reality.

May Lyndon's story, told through Jacci's strength and courage, be the legacy that saves lives.

INTRODUCTION

TRIGGER WARNING / DISCLAIMER

The events in this book are true and written based on my memory of events and personal opinion as a grieving widow and mother in a fight for life. I have backed up events with court judgements, where applicable.

I'd also like to take this opportunity to point out that I am not educated in any workplace health and safety (WH&S) or psychology field. I certainly do not write this book for people to feel sorry for me, but rather, out of my personal journey and lived experience, to show you that, whatever tragedy you get dealt with (and, unfortunately, I am sure you all will at some point in your life), you CAN choose to face the adversity with courage and resilience. I sure as hell know that is what Lyndon would want for me and our beautiful children.

For the purposes of this book, I do not mention everyone by name or I have changed certain people's names. This is purely out of respect and privacy for these people, who have lived through tragedy themselves, either by losing a loved one, being involved in, or witnessing such tragedy. Certain people I have named as they are aware that I have written about them.

"We are like books. Most people only see our cover, the minority read only the introduction, many people believe the critics. Few will know our content."

– ÉMILE ZOLA

My name is Jacqueline (Jacci) Quinlivan. I am a 40-year-old mum of two amazing children and a widowed wife to a husband who now has his angel wings. I reside in sunny Queensland, Australia, and am becoming quite the natural when it comes to navigating life's barriers and obstacles that get flung our way. I have definitely been through a few.

There are so many individuals who think they know our story, including what goes on behind closed doors. But the harsh reality is that only my children and I know, truly, what goes on. I chose the above quote because it resonates deeply within me, for various reasons, which you are about to read, and one of these is that our lives became very public after a workplace incident in 2018.

I live a normal life. I work a normal job, currently in a large education organisation as an Administration Officer, which I absolutely love (although currently work only on a contract). At the same time, I am also very proud to run my own growing business where I get to go out to industries and companies and meet like-minded people, just like yourself. I talk to them about safety in a workplace setting and what the harsh consequences are when you get it wrong. And, unfortunately, these can be dire. I believe I am helping to change the safety realm, albeit at a very slow pace.

In this book, I am going to an extremely vulnerable place whilst opening up my world, well, most of it, to give you a glimpse of what it's like to be us. It is my aspiration that you will be better equipped to have more of an understanding to not lay judgement on anybody. This is because the only person who is entitled to lay judgement on one's life is oneself.

This book was made to be a product of his legacy in a tangible form, and for me, it is a step further that adds a promise to myself that I can do anything that I set out to do. I will not sugarcoat the fact that this book has been difficult to write. At the same time, however, it has provided an "out" when I had so much turmoil going through my already strained and overloaded brain. Why, you may ask? Because Lyndon's legacy gave me the focus and determination to get this book written and ultimately published for my late husband, whom I made a promise to. Therefore, it is my legacy, too, that I want to leave for my family.

This book is like a diary of my life with the ebbs and flows, ups and downs, good times and very bad ones. I wanted to share my journey with the world so readers can take away meaning from different aspects of my life that they may resonate with, for whatever reason. I personally think that adversity strikes far too often. It hits all of us at some point in our lives, but trying to overcome it with resilience, grit and determination is ultimately what this book is all about.

At the end of each chapter, I will try to give a moment of reflection and/or learnings. Hopefully, they will help enable you to think about your own life from a different perspective. There will be questions to consider, thus turning the focus around to YOU and YOUR choice of how you would deal if you were faced with similar situations or scenarios.

I do not really know the type of genre this book would fall under; however, I think it would be a hybrid or combination of biography, autobiography, and maybe a little self-help. The best thing here is to let you have a read for yourself, then you can come to your own conclusion. In the next chapter, we'll dive straight into our personal lives while hopefully giving you a clearer understanding of my message - my WHY for writing this book.

Without further ado, my warrior friends, sink your teeth in and get reading. I have complete faith that you will take away something from this, even if it is just that you are not alone in this big, wide world. Have faith and trust that your heart and inner-voice will guide you - you just need to listen to it.

Jacci Q
XOXO

CHAPTER 1

MY PASSION = YOUR LEGACY

"Carve your name on hearts, not tombstones. A legacy is etched into the minds of others and the stories they share about you."

\- SHANNON L. ALDER

Shannon L. Alder couldn't have said it better and I strongly believe that is what I am doing right now in writing this and creating a legacy. This is a bloody big deal for me. It has taken a number of years to come to fruition, but after the long, tedious wait, **Endurance – A Widow's Insight into Workplace Tragedy**, has finally been born by way of a tangible product. This is just one of the numerous names that I tossed around for my very first book. I toyed with copious titles to get to the very one that had the best ring to it, whilst also encapsulating what this book actually represents - true endurance, hardships, resilience, love, and growth.

I played with "A belly full of fire", "Lyndon's Legacy", "Jacci's Journey from Lyndon's Legacy (JJLL)", "It wasn't just rotten eggs", "Lyndon's Voice", "Love Lives On", "Turning pain into passion", and even "H2S – I'm sour about it."

I have said from day one that I am my late husband's, Lyndon's, voice. I should make a recording of this line as I speak those words all too often. I nominated myself to speak up on his behalf because he no longer has that ability to do so. I also knew that, as his wife, I would never give up on my promise. I have been asked all sorts of questions about why I do what I do, and, honestly, the answer for me is very simple: his life was taken needlessly and unnecessarily at work, so that right for him to speak up was abruptly taken away.

Honouring Lyndon's legacy is my absolute and heartfelt vow. This is to ensure that his memory remains ever so active in my family's world and minds, because it matters most. Lyndon's legacy propels and pushes me forward each day. It forces me to share our very raw and very unfiltered story with as wide an audience as humanly possible. It is this mission alone that underpins and stresses the absolute significance of safeguarding others and preventing any other family from enduring the pain, torture, and torment that we have been met with and are still confronting to this day. It is what we will live with for our remaining days on this earth. Lyndon is on our minds constantly; he always will be! What I am choosing, however, is to flick the switch and turn my pain into passion whilst advocating for the safety of others. I have chosen hope above helplessness. Advocacy above adversity. Strength over suffering.

I have always aspired to author a book with the aim of helping and guiding others, and, ultimately, saving lives. My desire for this started in 2006 when, at the age of 21, I was going through my own medical challenges. I did not get there because, I guess you could say, the self-doubt spoke ever so sternly. After that, I did what a lot of people do, I listened to my inner critic and continued with the plan that life had for me.

The idea popped back into my head again in 2018, when the most challenging of situations - Lyndon's death - was thrust upon us as a family and obliterated our lives. If all I do from this is help just one person or save just one life, I would consider it a complete success. When I was a teenager suffering with mental health issues, I read a book by Susan Jeffers called "**Feel the Fear and Do it Anyway**." What better thing to do than to take and follow this advice? To fight against all the odds and fear that were against me and just do it anyway!

But, like most of you reading this, the self-doubt started to creep back in, leading me to ponder the many reasons not to proceed with such an outrageous idea. In those moments, it completely overwhelmed me. It froze me. "Who in their right mind would really want to listen to my voice?" "I'm a nobody!" "My life story and lived experience have no credit." Imposter syndrome alarm bells were chiming at their loudest. I was in a dark place, so naturally, the negative and damaging thoughts in my head were being fed and the critical thoughts kept coming, harsh and fast.

Now, however, I realise the value and significance of sharing my life story and experiences with the world. This book won't be for everyone; however, it's a narrative that, in my eyes, deserves to be heard. It is my goal that readers will find valuable snippets in this book that will assist them during their own challenging or trying times, potentially aiding others facing similar adversities. This may be in your personal or working life, and it is about finding the strength and courage to carry on and come out through the other side.

One of the most inspirational people I have met (you will hear about him later in this book) has coached me every step of the way in this book-writing journey. Even though I have always known deep down that I had the ability to write, he has helped, guided, and pushed me outside of my comfort zone to overcome that debilitating self-doubt and lack of confidence. I believe that's because he heard the potential that this story had and how much it needed to be shared with others. For that, Mr. A, I am eternally grateful.

In 2025, as I write this, my perspective and point of view on my family's "new normal" have evolved extensively from what I imagined during the struggles of 2006, 2018, and, naturally, the years that followed. The current state of my everyday life is a testament to adaptation and growth amidst adversity. Now, when I look ahead, I predict further transformation and growth as I pass through life's barriers; however, this time I am determined to not only survive, but flourish alongside my amazing family and in Lyndon's honour. I know that Lyndon is looking down from the heavens above with a smile beaming from ear to ear (holding a beer, of course) whilst saying, "That's my girl."

My wish is that our children look up to me, their mother, as a person who never gave up the fight no matter how hard it was. Even when her husband, and their father, was taken needlessly, and far too soon, in a workplace incident that was 100% preventable. For me, it is imperative for our children to witness firsthand how resilient we are together and how speaking up to fight a battle is the right thing to do for their father and for them.

It is my desire for them to be confident when they say, "That is my mum. We are so very proud of all that she has achieved since losing Dad." I want them to show this to their children one day and say, "Your nanna is an inspirational woman". Yes, you heard it first here, kids. WHEN I become a grandmother, I have already claimed the title of NAN, okay?

Martin Luther said, "If you want to change the world, pick up your pen and write." And that, my friends, is exactly what I am hoping to achieve now.

I have to say that I have been through the absolute ringer in my personal life. And Lyndon's death is the worst thing in my world (and my kids' world) to happen. But what I can also say with certainty is that so many people are still facing the worst time in their own lives, and there are still so many people worse off than me. Now I am not talking about trivial, petty, or meaningless and unimportant things, such as burnt toast, but more so the events that completely change our lives. You will read about mine shortly, but for you it could be something entirely different that is the biggest thing YOU have ever been through, and that, my friend...is...okay!

I am a firm believer that it is how someone reacts to those circumstances and situations that can bring out the most in an individual and, ultimately, their character.

Ever since 2018, I have not really been able to pick up a book and read as my concentration levels just are not there anymore. The irony is that writing this book has given me a form of therapy. In fact, I have thoroughly benefitted from it, despite it being very difficult at times. Go figure!

A MOMENT OF REFLECTION

After going through everything I have gone through to date in my life, I would like to offer my key learnings that, I believe, made me a better person. Do not get me wrong, I am not perfect by a long shot. I have made some not-so-good decisions, but I still show up for myself and others who play an important part in my world. I am indeed a human, just like you!

My hope is to educate, whilst at the same time, encouraging you to think or respond to situations differently, leading to personal growth amidst adversity.

They all say that you learn each day and change your perceptions as you continue to experience life. This is all extremely true, and although I have experienced a lot in my life, my key learnings are what make me who I am today.

REFLECTION QUESTIONS:

1. If you were authoring a book on your life, what would it be called and why?

2. What if I told you, **you have it in you** to use your voice and educate the people who need it most? Would you believe me? What would you use your voice for?

3. What is the absolute worst thing/s that has happened in your life to date, and how do you believe you have managed it?

4. With the same question in mind, if you had your time over, unfortunately still having been dealt the same shitty cards, what would you choose to do differently in response to the situation and why?

Jacci taken in 2023

CHAPTER 2

A TEENAGE ROMANCE BLOSSOMED INTO FOREVER

"You'll be the prince and I'll be the princess. It's a love story, baby, just say, 'Yes.'"

- TAYLOR SWIFT

We met on a platform called ICQ, late in the year 2000. I think it was December. ICQ was an internet instant messaging program that was founded in 1996, in the same good ol' days of Yahoo! chat rooms. It makes me feel quite old to be writing this today because I am now 40 years old, and when we met, I was only fifteen, whilst he was eighteen years old.

My memory of the first time I met with Lyndon is ever so clear - his attractive nervousness that gave away his introverted personality. The interaction between both introverts and extroverts often sparks the opinion of a perfect pair - isn't that what some people say? I remember that I was very nervous myself, but as an extrovert, I hid that part well (or so I thought). I recall thinking how "put together" he was; however, after meeting him for the first time, we both went our separate ways for approximately one month. Perhaps he did not like me? Maybe I am not his type? Of course, those were the thoughts running through my head, as the overthinker I was, and still am, although I kept on keeping on.

Reminiscing on the great times now gone past, I can say we were only young spring chickens. Who could have "thunk it" that we were about to experience a ride-of-a-lifetime kind of romance? Certainly not I. People nowadays are shocked when I tell them that I met Lyndon on the internet back in those days (the olden days if you ask my kids – like we are 80 years old or something). Remember the days of the dial-up internet? It was not that long ago. In my mind, I can still hear the sound of the dial-up modem screeching as it did. Back then, kids could not really sneak onto the internet without that loud sound or without disconnecting the phone line, sometimes when other family members were using it. Sorry for those inconvenient times, Mum! I think the kids of today really do have it easy compared to then.

Lyndon and I started chatting again in early 2001 and decided to meet up at the local swimming hole and I was rather fond of him, so much so, that I decided I was not holding back in my flirting abilities. We almost instantly became inseparable, on the days he was not working, of course.

He had just landed a new job, working at a local mill, which produced newsprint (newspaper) and he was so proud to be able to say where he worked. If you were known to work out there, you were held in pretty high esteem, so we later found out. Everybody wanted to work there, to be honest. It was one of the largest employers in the region. We lived in the township of Albury-Wodonga, and for anybody who does not know where that is, it is basically one of the largest towns between Sydney and Melbourne in Australia, straddling the NSW and Victorian border.

Lyndon's newly acquired job was shift work, where they worked a shift pattern of 4 days on and 4 days off. This typically equated to 2 nightshifts of 12 hours (7pm to 7am) with half a day off in between (known by employees as a "Clatan's day") and 2 dayshifts of 12 hours (i.e. 7am to 7pm).

His new job had its advantages. However, being a shift-worker also came with disadvantages, too, as their roster was generally set in stone. This was an operation that worked 365 days per year, which meant some years they would have to work Christmas Day or night, Easter, and New Year's. But he swiftly got used to that pattern, and as our lives further entwined, I did too. It was just routine now in our everyday family life. His father also worked there, so he knew the shift patterns well before he started, as well as the impact that shift work played on other family members of the household.

By now, I was (sweet?) sixteen and we had taken the first step in setting up the rest of our lives by moving in together. We moved into a tiny one-bedroom unit in East Albury, and that was the start of our amazing journey in spending the rest of our lives together.

It is the little things I try to remember now - like pushing my double bed up the road late at night as our new unit was just around the corner from where I had been living. The bed base was on castors (wheels). So we decided we would be smart (maybe not such a smart decision when looking back) and just push it up the road whilst laughing our heads off at how silly it must look and sound right now. I can still see the beautiful yet cheeky smile on his face and hear his contagious laugh.

He lit up the room with his laughter. I was recently telling our daughter about the things like this we got up to when we were younger. She said, "I could see you and Dad doing something like that," with a cheeky grin on her face. That exact same cheeky grin her father used to have.

At 16 years old, I commenced my career working full-time as a Trainee Receptionist at a local accounting firm in Wodonga. I think from memory, the correct terminology in my employment contract was "DOFI," which stood for Director of First Impressions. That was my first real job in the workforce. Who would have thought I would stay in the finance industry my whole working career, with only a short break trying another industry, until late 2022?

In Lyndon's spare time, he thoroughly enjoyed the sport of Ten Pin Bowling, where he bowled in a team league each week. He was an avid bowler, well before we even met, and regularly went away for bowling tournaments with his mates and people from the bowling community. Bowling certainly had a noticeably big piece of Lyndon's heart, and he was, undoubtedly, exceptionally good at it. He was one of those lucky people that was good at everything he attempted - no word of a lie. His hand-eye coordination was spot on. He had "a bee's dick accuracy," I remember his best mate saying one day. He even got me into the bowling sport, and I grew to love it just as much. His mother was also a keen bowler, and it became a shared piece of all our lives.

I had my own bowling shoes, single bowling bag and a lovely deep purple ball with glitter all through it. I still have it to this very day, would you believe. I think I stopped counting when Lyndon had collected about ten bowling balls. He was so into it, he had a different ball for different lane conditions. Yes, it's a real big thing in the bowling community, and they are extremely competitive when you get to tournament level. It makes me smile and chuckle when I think back to the times we would talk about "his balls" so openly. It's kind of a funny joke and anyone who is a bowler would understand this.

Before children, I would often accompany the men's team annually for their "Victorian Country Cup" bowling tournament. We would travel to towns like Ballarat, Bendigo, Mildura, and Warrnambool, just to name a few. I loved going with him and watching Lyndon's love of the sport grow each year.

Every day, we grew stronger and fiercer as a united couple. It was like I was living in a real-life fairytale. My childhood was not the best from the memories I do have, so how could everything at that time have been so amazingly perfect? People say no relationship is ever perfect, but I beg to differ. I am testament to a perfect relationship and marriage. Yes, of course we had our arguments (I'm not that naive), but we had this rule where we would NEVER go to sleep on an argument and we always honoured that – no matter what. Ultimately, I think that is why we worked everything out and were always such a united team. I had his back and he had mine. We loved each other unconditionally, and for that, I will be forever appreciative and grateful that I have experienced that kind of love. Because I know how rare that is.

We built our first home in Thurgoona, NSW, a suburb of Albury. At that time, I was 16 and he was 19. A charming little three-bedroom house set on a decent-sized block on a beautiful street at the end of a cul-de-sac, not far from all the amenities we needed. Our home backed onto a little park and walkway. It was perfect. We had just set our future family up and we were absolutely loving life.

Still at the age of 16 and 19 years old, we decided to get our first tattoos together. Lyndon was not one who was fond of needles, so there were a few hairy moments. But we grabbed chips from the local KFC that was right through the car park at the time, so we were set with a distraction. Lyndon got a dragon that was so lifelike it looked like it was crawling up his arm towards his shoulder. Whereas I got a nice petite butterfly crawling on a rose on my shoulder. At the age of 40, mine is looking a little worse for wear. I will get around to getting it touched up as it means a lot nowadays.

Once again, it is all those great memories that I often think about. A few years later, he got the Holden racing team (HRT) logo tattooed as Lyndon was Holden mad! We even named each of our dogs in the Holden theme:

- Monaro
- Maloo
- Storm (belonging to Lyndon's parents)
- Diesel

A few more years passed by, and then we were engaged. Yes, he got down on one knee down by the river after a romantic evening at the local cinema and proposed the old-fashioned way. He even asked my stepdad for my hand as that was the kind of person he was. He hid the preparations very well, as I had no idea. And, of course, I said YES. We marked this event with an engagement party at our house with all our important friends and family. And everything went off without a hitch. Again, it could not have been any more perfect in our eyes.

More years just breezed past whilst we were enjoying our young lives. That was until just shy of my 21st birthday. I had recently secured a new job as a Strata Manager, which was around the beginning of July 2006. This new venture was completely different from the finance industry I had always been in and known, but I must have felt that it was my time to do something different. I was excited; we were excited. We were about to embark on this new chapter of our lives together! Or so we thought. We certainly did not foresee what was about to transpire next.

A MOMENT OF REFLECTION

Reminiscing about those days as still young children ourselves, I realise that is what shaped me and even us as a young couple. You CAN choose to be happy, and honestly, you DESERVE happiness, because everyone does. There is nobody that I do not wish happiness upon.

> You will often hear me talking about practising gratitude for even the smallest of things. It is said that if you practise gratitude, it causes the focus to be positive even in negative experiences. Thus raising resilience through adversity and the rough times. It cannot hurt to try, right? All you need to do is think about the positive things.

REFLECTION QUESTIONS:

1. Reflect on your own relationships (be they romantic or not), are you 100% happy and satisfied? If not, grow a pair and do something about it because nobody is coming to save you.

2. For my relationship, it was enormously about never going to sleep on an argument that I believe fully grounded us. What is one thing that you would choose to ground your relationships in?

3. What happened today for which you are grateful? (This could be as simple as "the sun shining.")

4. Who is one person that you are grateful for having in your life? Send them a thank you message or do one better by picking up the phone and calling them.

Lyndon - Looking beautiful in his teenage years

Lyndon - Young and Carefree

Lyndon & Jacci - Bright, Victoria in 2002

Young Love - Lyndon & Jacci, 2003

CHAPTER 3

ADVERSITY HIT US HARD!

"In the face of adversity, you find out if you are a fighter or a quitter. It's all about getting up after you've been knocked down."

– ARCHIE GRIFFIN

Most people will remember happy memories of their 21st birthday party. But for me, instead of the joyful and positive memories such an occasion would bring, the memories are full of distress and anxiety. This weekend, in 2006, we held a very small, intimate celebration with a few close friends and family at a local hotel restaurant. It was wonderful seeing everyone, and things were going off just as they were supposed to.

I had one alcoholic beverage this night. I was not much of a drinker at the best of times, so no alarm bells were going off. I guess, when I was slightly younger, I did a lot of drinking. So perhaps I got it out of my system? I did drink, do not get me wrong, but I just did not feel the desire to get blind drunk for my 21st.

In the early hours of the following morning, we got in a taxi and made our way home (nope, I don't believe Ubers were a thing yet). A couple of friends were staying at our house, and more friends were camped in their caravan on our front lawn. So it was safe to say our house was a hive of activity.

That morning, Lyndon woke me and I recall telling him that I had a bad headache and just wanted to sleep. He told me to sleep for a bit longer, but not for too long as we had visitors. An hour or so passed and he tried waking me again. He told me I really needed to get up because we had people over and it may seem rude. I still had a migraine-like headache, so he said he would help me into the shower and that may make me feel better. I tried to stand up, but immediately fell to the floor. It was at that moment that Lyndon knew something was drastically wrong.

At only 24 years old, he certainly did not think of the worst. I mean, who would when you are young, healthy, and active? I can still recall the walk from our bedroom to his car in our driveway. He basically guided me, as I had my eyes closed because the light was so painful. He somehow put me into his car and drove me straight to the emergency department of our closest local hospital. What became apparent next was never in our future plans.

I do not remember too much from here on in, but what I do remember was the migraine. I had never before suffered from one before, so it was all very scary. I do not remember the walk from the hospital carpark into the emergency department waiting room. However, I do recall they had a dark, quiet room to put me in until the doctor arrived to triage and assess me. By the time I was seen to, I recall that my thoughts were not connecting with my mouth.

I remember them asking me, "Do you know where you are?"

I mumbled something along the lines of "Yeah, I'm in Thurgoona hospital."

But as those words were leaving my mouth, I knew there was no hospital in Thurgoona, but I could not stop it. Looking back, it is a scary thought when your brain is not synced with your mouth and a jumbled mumble is spurting out.

Lyndon was trying to tell the doctors and nurses that this is very out of character for me. I felt that they were judging me – I mean, I just turned 21 and went out for a party the night before. I think the general assumption made by many involved drugs or a spiked drink. One would, however, hope that the medical fraternity does not make assumptions or judgements like this and would base their assessments on facts alone. But I wholeheartedly feel that I was placed into a certain category.

They were saying things to my fiancé.

"Has she had ants crawling all over her body?"

"Could she have done drugs without you knowing?"

"Perhaps she had her drink spiked."

But Lyndon kept saying the same thing: No, she does not do drugs. No, she only had one drink. No, she is not crazy... He was becoming very tired of the assumptions, as you could probably imagine.

They did try sending me home just after. But, thankfully, my mother-in-law-to-be came to support both Lyndon and me. She told them, very sternly I might add, that I was in absolutely no state to go home and something was seriously wrong. I was attempting to stand, and that is when I lost complete movement of my right side. My arm and leg were not working and my face had drooped. Poor Lyndon was beside himself, watching me go through that and feeling so helpless. I know he loved me so much, and I also know that it almost broke him. I thank the Lord that he had his mum's support during that scary time in both of our lives.

Whilst still in emergency at the time, I lost yet another part of me – my dignity! Can you ever imagine, at 21 years old, needing full assistance to go to the bathroom? I mean FULL assistance. That help obviously came in the form of nurses, but predominantly from my fiancé and his mother. At this stage, you would surely think something is seriously wrong, right?

Maybe they were. But it really felt to me that because I had been placed in this category, they were not focusing on the all-important FAST rule when it comes to the possibility of a stroke. The doctors decided to now order a CT scan. This showed nothing abnormal from memory, and the doctors just presumed that I was better placed in the psychiatric ward. To this day, it still scares me how easily these opinions are formed. Naturally, I do not have faith in a great deal of the medical fraternity based on my experience.

The registrar from the psych ward was asked to come and do an assessment of me. I am eternally grateful for him as he said something along the lines of "I don't believe she belongs in my ward, please send her for an MRI scan and I will only take her if nothing significant shows up."

The next thing I knew, I was being loaded into an ambulance and on my way to another hospital, as that was where the MRI machine was located. Lo and behold, it apparently lit up like a Christmas tree.

At the tender age of just 21, I had officially suffered an ischemic stroke. Unfortunately for me, I could not take any clot-busting medication as I was already outside the window of time for it to work. I was told I may have presented originally with a transient ischemic attack

(TIA) and then had the actual stroke in the hospital. That series of events is something I have had very serious and significant trauma over. Only recently, July, 2025 to be precise, am I trying to work through those events with my amazing psychologist, and I have started EMDR therapy for this and other traumatic life events. Little did I know at the time, the whole experience set me on the path towards helping others facing similar adversity.

Later on, I discovered this quote by Archie Griffin and this quote has resonated deeply with me ever since.

> *"In the face of adversity, you find out if you are a fighter or a quitter. It's all about getting up after you've been knocked down."*

From then on, knowing the diagnosis, I was able to get the help I needed to return to our new, but soon normal, life. Lyndon now had the challenging task of phoning my mother to let her know the devastating news. Mum was living in the United States of America at the time, so you may be able to empathise with her and the array of emotions she must have been feeling after learning that her daughter was dealt such a blow. She arranged the earliest possible flight to be with us.

Many tests later (yes, I was a pin cushion for months), they were still unable to find the cause with certainty. I believe that is what is known as a "cryptogenic" stroke. They put it down to my contraceptive pill and a small hole they found in my heart, which they believe contributed to the clot travelling to my brain. I was transferred by plane to a hospital in Melbourne to have the hole (medically known as a patent foramen ovale or PFO) closed. However, they said it was very small and decided they were going to leave it. So, I still have the hole in my heart to this very day, and naturally, this is still a big concern I have. After a few days in Melbourne, I was transported by road back to the local hospital, where I was then placed in the rehabilitation ward.

It took a few days of being in the rehabilitation ward to get (slightly) well enough to return home. I was the youngest by far in the hospital, but I made friends with a few of the nurses and patients. As the youngest patient among them, my road to recovery journey served as a source of inspiration, revealing the path to resilience and a sense of renewal for those around me. In the midst of my own struggles, I discovered the intense power of offering hope and encouragement to others even in the darkest of times, yet I did not even realise it. It is in these moments of shared strength that true empowerment emerges, shaping a narrative of strength, spirit, and unity. I thought, at the time, I would author a book on this life event, but never got around to it as life got in the way. After surviving the stroke, and coming out of the hospital sometime later, I experienced a profound shift in my perception of life. The feeling of invincibility washed over me, giving me the courage to navigate the road ahead with newfound strength. Despite the challenges of my recovery, where progress seemed painstakingly slow, I found solace in being a symbol of hope for others on the ward.

I remember one resident, who was my roommate, a lovely woman named Betty. Betty was in for a bit of respite. She had Motor Neurone Disease (MND). She would often sit in the lunchroom with her friends, playing cards. One particular day, she asked me if I wanted to join in, and that is when my love for the card game, Five Crowns, was born. We have since shown a lot of our family and friends, who have, in turn, bought a deck and shown their family and friends. All that was due to Betty's love of cards. Unfortunately, I later found out the disease took her, but I am forever grateful to have met such a wonderful and inspiring woman.

Thank you, Betty. I am sure you are up there playing cards with Lyndon.

Then I transitioned to being an outpatient, attending the hospital to do the rehab and physio I needed. As an outpatient, I then had to try and work out what our new normal looked like. A while after that, we collaborated with amazing people to assist my journey of transitioning me back into the workforce. It really was a hard, bloody slog. To this day, 19 years on, I still have side effects from my stroke and severe trauma. Not many people know this, as I believe I hide it well, but my trauma from having that stroke has not subsided over time, and the fear has only gotten worse.

That year, for my 21st birthday, Lyndon had bought me a stunning gold belcher bracelet that he had engraved. I had always wanted one of these, and it looked even more beautiful on my wrist than I could have ever imagined. I wore it out to my 21st party, and due to what occurred, I have never been able to wear it again. Why? Because that was one of the scariest times in my life, and I still cannot bring myself to do anything that brings up those memories. I have never been back to the place we went for dinner, and the thought of it makes me feel sick to the stomach. I do, however, have my beautiful bracelet in my jewellery box, and each time it's opened, I get a wonderful reminder of that perfect present from Lyndon.

After numerous doctors' visits over many years, in early 2023, my current GP took seriously my concerns for early-onset Parkinson's and referred me to see a local neurologist. I thought this was a good opportunity as I did not have a specialist in that field since we lived in Albury, so off I toddled to my appointment.

When I entered his rooms, it was evident he hadn't looked over my chart beforehand as he asked, "How can I help?"

I simply said, "I think I may have Early-Onset Parkinson's!"

You could see his brain cogs start turning and he very quietly chuckled, which I thought a bit rude. He then proceeded to ask what my symptoms were, and so I rattled them off. He again looked puzzled and then replied with "Well, you'd have to be very unlucky."

I guess on this day I wasn't feeling my normal bubbly and positive self, and replied with, "You want to talk about luck?" which I thought was a pretty witty reply, and rattled off the number of unlucky things I had dealt with, with the stroke at the top of the list.

"Oh, you've had a stroke?" he asked.

Ummm, that is what I just said.

"We will perhaps send you for a CT scan of your brain," he said.

My reply was, "I'll do one better, I had one a few months ago. You can take a look at that."

He grabbed my details and asked a few questions pertaining to my history and scheduled a follow up appointment in a couple of weeks. I came out of there feeling rather puzzled and muddled because I hadn't had an answer for so long. But now it felt like he was taking me seriously, after feeling initially he was taking the piss out of me. 2 weeks later, I was back in his office for the follow-up.

"Well," he said, "I have good news – you don't have Parkinson's. However, you DO appear to have Parkinson's symptoms," he explained.

He proceeded to bring up the image of my brain on the CT scan and show me the section that "died" when I suffered the stroke back in 2006. It was actually the section of the brain that can affect a Parkinson's patient. He finished off by saying, "So you may just have some symptoms, but rest assured there's no disease. However, because that part of your brain is 'dead', medication may not work, should we ever need to go down that route."

What the actual hell was I listening to? I had just gotten a new diagnosis all these years later! I certainly don't recall them telling me back in 2006 that this was the part of the brain that was affected, and it may or may not cause other issues later in life. These are trivial things in the grand scheme, and I always try to look at the glass half full, but I really had to dig deep when I learnt this news, that's for sure. Even writing and re-living this, digging deep is what I need to remember for my own sanity. Having a brain injury is a really hard pill to swallow!

The latest symptom began in May, 2025, the imminent lead up to Lyndon's death anniversary, and I got slight eye twitching. This year, I was extremely stressed, and it was getting so bad that I'd have it for hours at a time and usually more than once a day. After the 24th and 25th May (you will read about the significance of these dates later), the eye twitching stopped a lot, but it is still there. According to Dr Google, this is another small symptom of Parkinson's. I'm learning to just go with the flow nowadays, and I am ever so grateful for my amazing psychologist, as I wouldn't be able to manage my mental health struggles without her.

A MOMENT OF REFLECTION

It has taken me almost 20 years post-stroke to come to terms with the amount of trauma I have built up in my system. I am grateful, however, I have now found an amazing therapist who brought this to light and is collaborating hard with me to work through my issues.

Trauma, depression, PTSD, and other mental illnesses are NOT a weakness. If I can seek help after all these years, anyone can! I passionately believe everybody needs a psychologist or councillor throughout their lives to talk through important things that come up.

Nobody, and I mean **nobody,** is immune to the shitty cards we all get dealt with whilst we are on this journey called life. We need to talk about mental health. It should not be a taboo subject. I am a firm believer that anybody who wishes to minimise or make fun of somebody else's mental health issues is the person who is fighting the darkest demons. Can we make a mental health movement so people dealing with this do not feel so alone?

How amazing that would be! Let us normalise speaking up about issues, thus potentially helping somebody in the dark depths of depression, trauma, and PTSD. **#mentalhealthmovement**

REFLECTION QUESTIONS:

1. Have a think (you may need to dig deep) about a time of adversity in your own life. Has any resilience come of it that has given or could give hope to others?

2. Stroke can happen to anyone at any age. Once you are aware of that, the number of people you hear about who "were young" is scary. Always be aware of the FAST acronym when it comes to stroke: Face, Arms, Speech, and Time. By using this acronym, you may just be able to identify the symptoms of a stroke thus potentially saving your life.

3. Don't think it can not happen to you (whatever IT may be). Stay vigilant. And if you are in a hospital setting, **fight for your rights**. Trust your gut!

CHAPTER 4

OUR AMAZING WEDDING

"Love is a partnership of two unique people who bring out the very best in each other, and who know that even though they are wonderful as individuals, they are EVEN better together."

– BARBARA CAGE

Our big day was fast approaching with excitement filling the air. We were getting more excited by the day. We thought that after all the challenges we had been through over the last year, we surely deserved some happy times. We knew those times were indeed just around the corner and eagerly anticipated them. The reality was we were really getting married, yet still it seemed like a fairytale.

Every ounce of our dream day was planned, meticulously thought out in detail. Planning a wedding can be stressful at the best of times, but ensuring a perfect day truly trumps and makes it more worthwhile. Perhaps I could even put wedding planning on my resume? Nah. Looking back, the memories just amaze me each and every time. Reminiscing about how young we were. Oh, how beautiful we both were. Oh, how in love we were and always would be!

The anniversary of the date that we officially became a couple was 10 February, 2001. Now, being a female, most of us know that most guys (not all guys) are not as date-driven to remember any more anniversaries than are needed, right? So, lo and behold, I had a light bulb moment to pick out this same date for our wedding. Of course, the idea resonated with Lyndon, too. 2007 was the next time February 10 fell on a Saturday. Excitedly, we both agreed that February 10, 2007, would be our special day of becoming Mr and Mrs Quinlivan.

Now that we had the date set in stone, it was time to get to the planning of this special day. I was your typical bride on a mission to have everything P.E.R.F.E.C.T. I certainly was not a bridezilla, as was the famous word of the month back then. Our first thing to do was to create an (extraordinarily long) to-do list so that we could tick items off one by one and watch our progress. By this time, I had a pretty good collection of wedding magazines, which aided in making those larger choices just ever so slightly easier. We attended a bridal expo which, from memory, was held at the Hume Weir, and, boy, what an experience that was! Who knew there was so much to plan for a wedding? We certainly were in shock, and it was not until we had to start booking our vendors that we realised just how much of a waitlist they all had.

So much thought and care naturally go into such an event that until you have gone through it, you cannot comprehend the level of complexity. Our guest list was large (for us) yet intimate, with around 120 guests from memory. I will not lie, it was taxing at times. Not because of the people we were inviting, but getting the all-important invitations sent out, creating the seating arrangements, and last-minute acceptances thus redoing the seating plans. Even details like working out who our marriage celebrant would be were big questions. Obviously, we had to settle on the menu plans before we ran out of time, but it was truly quite a cakewalk and very enjoyable. Writing our vows was slightly more challenging; however, it added that special Jacci and Lyndon touch to our already exceptional day.

Planning the reception tied into this complex planning, as you would imagine. At first, it was the nutting out of bigger decisions. Where was it to be held? Would they have the date we wanted? The table and chair dressings had to be arranged. Who would be our DJ and MC? Should we create a wedding gift registry? All of these preparations had to be undertaken; however, we were both ready for the challenge, as we were ready for a flawless celebration. And flawless it most certainly was, even if I am, ever so slightly, biased. In my opinion, it was the wedding of the century!

Another happy memory from the wedding preparations is how Lyndon carefully selected Holden cars, including a ute, which added a unique touch. It started off with Lyndon noticing the car on one of Albury's streets that he admired so much. So he left a note on the windscreen, to which he received a reply from the owner agreeing for it to be used for our wedding.

Our wedding cake selection was decided after an enjoyable and delicious taste test, leaving us to settle on a 3-tier mud cake. The pleasing part for us was that we were already confident in our cake decorator's skills, having previously had her bake and decorate our engagement party cake. The creativity of professional bakers never ceases to amaze me. My own cake-making skills only extend as far as a very obvious home-baker chocolate fondant with very messy, piped icing handwriting.

Off we went one day to do our wedding ring shopping. We always purchased our jewellery from one specific jeweller, so that choice was not made difficult. But the ring design was a little bit of a different story. We settled on some fantastic choices though, including an amazing two-toned ring with one diamond for Lyndon. For a bloke, he never ceased to amaze me with his choices as he did have incredibly good taste – I mean, he chose me, right? So, I guess I should not be so stunned, I think as I chuckle to myself writing this.

The exquisite engagement ring that he had chosen for me was absolute perfection. It was a yellow-gold 9ct gold ring with a princess cut diamond in the centre, wrapped by 3 smaller diamonds on each side. So, when it came to the wedding bands, I had already decided that I wanted split wedding bands to embrace each side of the engagement ring. And we found the absolute perfect pair of rings, which also had a band of diamonds across the top and lined up perfectly with my engagement ring. The purchase was made promptly so that we didn't miss the opportunity. As soon as we were married, we got my bands soldered together into one big band so they would not slip and slide.

Another unforgettable day, both my mother and Lyndon's joined me to go wedding dress shopping. It was an absolutely remarkable experience where I truly felt like a princess. The dream for my wedding dress was kind of unique - a variation on your traditional white bridal gown with black or burgundy stitching and lace. Do not ask me why, I just always had this image in my head since I was young. Well, all I can say is that after a few dresses were tried on, the absolute perfect dress (for me) just screamed out. It was a strapless dress in pure white with a white lace overlay. The bodice was close-fitting, then seamlessly flowed into a puffy A-line skirt. It was not what I had thought I would go for. However, I knew Lyndon would love it just as much as I did. Trying to keep my choice a secret for as long as I did was extremely difficult, as I was terrible at keeping anything secret from him. Obviously, I am glad I did because seeing his face light up as I walked down that aisle said it all, and his smile felt like home!

Shopping for a wedding dress is a memorable and unforgettable experience for every person who chooses to embark on such a journey. Thinking about this special day, I decided to have my beautiful wedding dress dry-cleaned and delicately boxed after the magical celebration. A choice I am now pleased about and extremely grateful for. It's moments like that which add to the precious recollections of such an exquisite celebration.

Our colour theme that we easily agreed upon was a pinkish tone. The bridesmaid dresses were a rusty-pink, strapless dress. I had three bridesmaids, including my sister-in-law and Lyndon's best man's (and best mate since school) wife, who was a particularly good friend. They looked absolutely drop-dead gorgeous and elegant, if I do say so myself.

The flowers were then selected. We opted for artificial flowers for various different yet specific reasons which predominantly were to be able to keep these as a memento of our special day. The other reason we chose this style was that the wedding was in February, the hottest time of the year here in Australia. Artificial flowers would definitely not wilt or look anything less than amazing.

The day had come at last and it was an absolute cracker of a day. We had opted for an outdoor ceremony. We loved the gardens, so it was a clear winning choice of the perfection of the Botanic Gardens situated in our hometown of Albury. The sun was shining, birds were chirping, and there was not a cloud in the sky. It was our day! The morning was a hive of activity in the hotel room. The makeup artists were arriving as well as our hairdresser who all worked attentively to ensure we all looked our absolute best. And I honestly couldn't have asked for a better outcome, because I felt like a true princess and so did the bridesmaids. The photographer was busy taking our pre-wedding photos - both the women getting ready and the boys, who were having just as fabulous a morning. The captured moments in our wedding photographs are equally mind-blowing for me, serving as everlasting keepsakes of that wonderful and cheerful occasion.

When the afternoon came, which we had been ever so patiently waiting for, I was placed into our main wedding car, where we embarked on the short 2-minute drive to our destination. I knew how incredibly fortunate I was. I was lucky enough to be able to walk (thinking about my stroke) down the aisle where I was given away by my stepdad to my beautiful, handsome-looking fiancé, very soon to become husband.

We held our reception at the Best Western Hovell Tree Inn in Albury, NSW. And it was just as luxurious as we could have ever imagined. Just writing this, I can still see the smile beaming from ear to ear on Lyndon's face, as well as the nice burn marks and holes on the knees of his hired suit pants from doing an Elvis Presley impersonation on the dance floor later that evening. We may have had a little much to drink, but we were overjoyed celebrating OUR day. Being able to share such a memorable day with our closest family and friends was an absolute privilege that I don't take for granted. I never remembered what happened when we returned those hired pants to the shop in their post-Presley impersonation condition. But whatever happened, our wedding day was so perfect that I don't care what the repercussions were - it was worth every cent!

We opted for the picturesque Gold Coast, Queensland, Australia, for our honeymoon to celebrate our youth and love. Beginning our journey by road from our hometown of Albury on the NSW/VIC border, it was approximately a 13-hour drive from point A to point B. On the way, we savoured a few tranquil days in Forster on the mid north coast and Coffs Harbour, which is well known as the home of the big Banana, before indulging in the beauty of the Gold Coast. Our adventures included exploring various attractions, with Dreamworld being a highlight of our memorable honeymoon. Oh, to be young again!

A MOMENT OF REFLECTION

Writing this and reminiscing of that wonderful and oh-so-perfect day, it again makes me think about all the things for which I am grateful. I will not lie, it makes me profoundly sad also, but I am so utterly grateful to have met and married the wonderful Lyndon Quinlivan. I am grateful I get to call him my husband. I am grateful for the beautiful life we have created together. I look back and I am grateful for so many things.

REFLECTION QUESTIONS:

1. What are you grateful for in your life (it can be anything at all, big or small)?

2. Perhaps start a gratitude journal. If you find yourself struggling to see the good in the world, this may help shift your perspective. Focus on the good, not just the bad.

3. Do you reminisce about the great times in your life that have now gone by?

4. Real love is out there for EVERYONE. Do not settle for anything less than you deserve. You owe this to yourself.

Engagement party - Best mates, Lyndon and Al

Lyndon & his sister on our wedding day

Our Engagement Party - Lyndon, Jacci and Lyndon's Parents

Engagement photo shoot, 2006. Photography by Peta

Our magical wedding day, 10 February, 2007

Our Engagement Party - Lyndon, Jacci & our two amazing mothers

Wedding Chocolate bars we gave each guest.
Yes, I still have it to this very day, almost 20 years on.
I would hate to see what the chocolate actually looks like now

Lyndon & Jacci on their wedding day. Photography by Peta

CHAPTER 5

COULD WE HAVE CHILDREN?

"One day you will be able to look into your baby's eyes and tell them about the incredible journey you went through to bring them into the world."

– NICOLA HEADLEY

We had talked about, in great detail, whether or not kids were even on the cards now because of my recent health scare and ongoing battles. In the beginning, we had planned to wait a little while and enjoy our newly married life as just the two of us, husband and wife, Lyndon and Jacci. As a result of my recent stroke, however, we understood firsthand how valuable and short life was and could be, so we thought we would try as soon as we were given the OK from our medical advisors. There were a lot of specialists involved, even travelling 2 hours to Melbourne to get specialist opinions. On reflection, knowing what I know now, I am extremely grateful that we made that decision.

We had a lot of medical appointments to see if I could even carry a child post stroke and, if so, what it would look like. But all in all, the medical advice was I could carry a child, but I would be deemed high risk and in the care of my medical team – who were absolutely fantastic by the way. My main obstetrician was, without a doubt, top tier.

It was a great surprise to us both at how quickly we fell pregnant, and even more exciting because we conceived on our honeymoon. Naturally, we were absolutely overjoyed and trying to contain our excitement proved difficult. It is incredible how quickly you get attached to something you know is growing inside of you. The happiness, however, just as quickly turned to tears and grief as I miscarried our first pregnancy. I wholeheartedly believe this event played a critical role in the anxiety-filled journey on which we had just embarked. We had not told many people yet, but knowing that I had a heartbeat inside me one minute and then didn't the next was extremely difficult to comprehend.

Together, however, we got through the miscarriage just like we always did through every other adversity. Whoever was constantly tossing those spanners towards us did not realise who they were dealing with. The miscarriage was yet another traumatic event to wade through whilst we continued growing stronger and stronger as a newly-married, young couple.

Evidently, we were both very fertile people (laugh aloud) as after another short while, we fell pregnant again. From memory, it was our first try. Again, we were overjoyed, just as you could imagine. Although ecstatic and over the moon, this time it was shadowed by immense fear. I was so frightened at every point in this pregnancy, every twinge, pain, or you name it. The time felt like it was passing at a snail's pace. But when that magical 12-week mark finally passed, we could rest our fears (mostly) and safely tell people. And we couldn't contain the excitement! I had always known I wanted to be a mother.

It was time for the gender scan, and we both could not wait, so we found out the sex. We were having a little boy! Both Lyndon and I were just in awe of each other and the little life we were creating. Watching him transition into preparing and becoming the best father was an absolute honour - another highlight of my life. As I was considered high risk by my medical team, as mentioned before, I had more obstetricians' appointments and scans than you could poke a stick at. But I certainly was not complaining. We got to see our precious baby boy each time and I knew we were in the best care possible.

We were talking about the impending birth and found out that they would let me attempt delivery naturally (no scheduled c-section). But as they did not want me to strain at all, I would have an epidural to play it safe. We were okay with this as we just wanted to ensure a safe delivery and healthy mum and baby boy at the conclusion.

At 36 weeks pregnant, I had to stop taking my blood-thinning medication (which I am on permanently to prevent any future strokes) and switch to daily injections of a different, safer blood-thinner. Even though we could have done it ourselves, neither Lyndon nor I could bring ourselves to inject into my big belly when I was so heavily pregnant, so we had a nurse come to our home daily at 11:00am to do the honours. Looking back, they were probably cursing us, but the thought of a needle hitting our son's head sent shivers up our spines. It just did not feel right. Then, just before 39 weeks when I was to be induced, I had to stop the blood-thinners altogether. The induction gave my medical team more control over the birth, which, obviously, in turn, was safe for both of us.

At 39 weeks, the night before I was due to head into the hospital to be induced, I woke to bad abdominal pains. I did not want to bother Lyndon as he was peacefully sleeping, and I gathered he would need all the sleep he could get, so I got up and lay on the couch. The pains were getting stronger, so I phoned my mother, who resided in America, and she said it sounds like I am in labour.

The excitement grew. The nerves were definitely there, but also sheer excitement. Every pain was amazing! I was not scared by the pains, it was thrilling. But I knew (by about 4am) that we better ring the hospital and I better wake Lyndon and get him out of bed. Lyndon woke excitedly, albeit nervously. We phoned the hospital and said I was due in at 6am, but I think I had gone into labour. They said to come straight over, so excitedly we got in the car and drove the 20 or so minutes across the state border into Victoria, where the hospital was (there were no birthing facilities in Albury.) We were both just as eager and excited as each other that we were finally going to meet our little bundle of joy!

I got to about 5cm dilated and, truth be told, by this stage I could not handle the pain. As soon as I said that, I had a needle in my back and I was epidural'ed up. I will be the first to admit it, pain is not my forte, and I guess you could say I am a bit of a sook.

My mother and sister-in-law stopped by the hospital, and it was so nice to see them. As I recall, I was not in any pain. I managed to catch a bit of shut eye a few times, but also vomited a few times, but it was just really a waiting game now. Time went by and a few pushes later, with the help of medical forceps and a few stitches, our precious baby boy was born! As soon as he arrived, he was rushed straight to the special care nursery for assistance as he wasn't breathing correctly and they needed to ensure he would be okay. He was okay. He was absolutely and utterly perfect. I was, in fact, quite calm while all this kafuffle was going on, because I knew deep down that he was perfect and he was safe with his daddy beside him.

We had not yet thought of a name. I remember all throughout the pregnancy when I would bring up the discussion about names, Lyndon would say "we've got plenty of time." And even when we were in the hospital pre-admission, in labour mind you, I brought it up again and got the same reply.

"We've got plenty of time."

Looking back now, it cracks me up how calm he was. After he was born, Lyndon said, "I guess we'd better talk about names."

I wanted to name him Beau. But as we were talking, Lyndon said, "Chris. Let's name him Chris and you can name our next one."

Not up for any discussions at that time as we were besotted with our bundle of joy, I agreed. So that's what we did. Chris was born on the 19th February 2008. A magical day I will never forget.

I remember my mother-in-law asking me very soon after Chris was born if I would do it all over again, and for me, the answer was a no-brainer. Abso-bloody-lutely I would! In a heartbeat. It really is true that as soon as your baby is born, love swells your heart, and you forget all pain. I could not wait to get pregnant again, no word of a lie.

Writing this book, I have naturally been incredibly open about a lot of things, and there are certainly things in here that even people close to us may not have known. One of those things was that I got diagnosed with PND, or postnatal depression, a while after our son Chris was born. I was extremely ashamed, and I was as confused as Lyndon. Confused at how or why I could be depressed whilst at the same time I couldn't be any more thrilled with our little family. I was so overprotective of our little boy, and although I had post-natal depression, I would not change anything. Not a single thing.

PND isn't something we cannot control. It was my body going through enormous bodily and hormonal changes. Having my husband was with me at every appointment being an amazing support person made the depression easier to treat and get me on the road to recovery. The statistics are 1 in every 5 new mothers are diagnosed with postnatal depression. Yet, even in today's day and age, people are still hesitant to talk about it.

We fell pregnant again a while later, and again, we suffered another miscarriage. Although miscarriage is quite common, when you experience it, no matter how far along you may be, it is nothing short of traumatic. My fears had just been reopened and elevated tenfold.

Not long after the 2nd miscarriage, we again were expecting (I did tell you, we were obviously very fertile people.) And extremely nervous was an understatement of how we felt. This theory that my body could not keep a fetus alive was in my brain, and I often beat myself up over this. The fear and emotional pain was eating me up inside.

This pregnancy felt different. I was sicker and very often vomiting over the smell of just about anything. We were so thrilled, however, to be able to give Chris a sibling and become a family of four. We both wanted 2 children, so our family was almost complete. I will not lie, though, the fear that I was holding on to (clearly not by choice) was almost too much to bear. At the 12-week ultrasound, we started telling everyone, and again, we opted to find out the sex when we could. At our gender scan, we found out we were having a little girl. We were over the moon!

Again, however, I was considered a high-risk patient, so I had to be monitored closely, and again I had to go off the blood-thinning medications, swapping to the blood-thinning injections at the 36-week mark. This time was different though. Because we had been through the injections before, we had to learn how to do it ourselves. There was no way in hell that Lyndon was going to inject me, so it was I who had to step up and take one for the team, first learning on an orange. Once I got the hang of it, it was quite easy to do. Needless to say, needles don't scare me anymore. Again, when I went in to be induced at 39 weeks, I was already about 3cm dilated, and they immediately broke my waters. It was all on like Donkey Kong from here on in.

For this birth, they decided they were going to let me see how far I could get, but again, if I needed relief, it was right there on standby. I was so excited. I got to about 5 or 6 centimeters, then said I couldn't do it (remember, I don't handle pain very well). I immediately was given the epidural. However, by the time they took the needle out of my back, I was already at 9, nearly 10cm, and ready to push, which means I still had some feeling and was in extreme pain. Our precious baby girl was born and she was perfect. True to our prior discussions of naming our children, I was the one who named our daughter Mia in September of 2009.

Poor Lyndon had the flu (swine flu, I think it was back then) when Mia was born. So he was slightly worse for wear. He gave Mia a big cuddle, then took himself to the doctor then home to sleep. We did not think he was allowed at the hospital, so he stayed away as that was the right thing to do. The nurse came in about 2 days later and asked where he was, so I told her. She said to get a mask for him and tell him to come straight in to spend that valuable time with his daughter. Mia and I got to see him within the hour.

I again suffered postnatal depression after Mia, but we knew the signs to be on the lookout for and sought help straight away. One thing I am grateful for, during both bouts of depression, is that it never took away from my amazing bonding experience with my two amazing babies.

We had the two most beautiful children and a pigeon pair at that. From the very moment both kids were born, Lyndon truly became our family man. Our family was complete!

A MOMENT OF REFLECTION

Growing up, I had always dreamed of becoming a mother, and I am so grateful I got the chance to experience that, as I am acutely aware that some people are not afforded that luxury. Even after everything life threw at us, we were able to conceive and raise our beautiful children. I am so grateful to my obstetrician and the whole medical team for providing me with the opportunity to experience this. Especially considering that at one point, we were unsure if we would ever be able to have kids of our own. I look at this and know, anything is possible.

The PND for me stemmed from the trauma-filled years before. I couldn't have foreseen this nor avoided it, but as with everything, you can learn from it.

REFLECTION QUESTIONS:

1. Did you know the rate of PND is as high as 1 in 5 mothers, but it also affects fathers at a rate of 1 in 10? Chances are, you have experienced this or certainly know of someone who has. This subject is still not commonly spoken of, and this needs to change.

2. If you have ever suffered PND after (or before) the birth of your child, please do not ever be ashamed. Talk about this shit openly, and let's get a movement happening so that nobody needs to feel like a failure for their body going through natural changes.

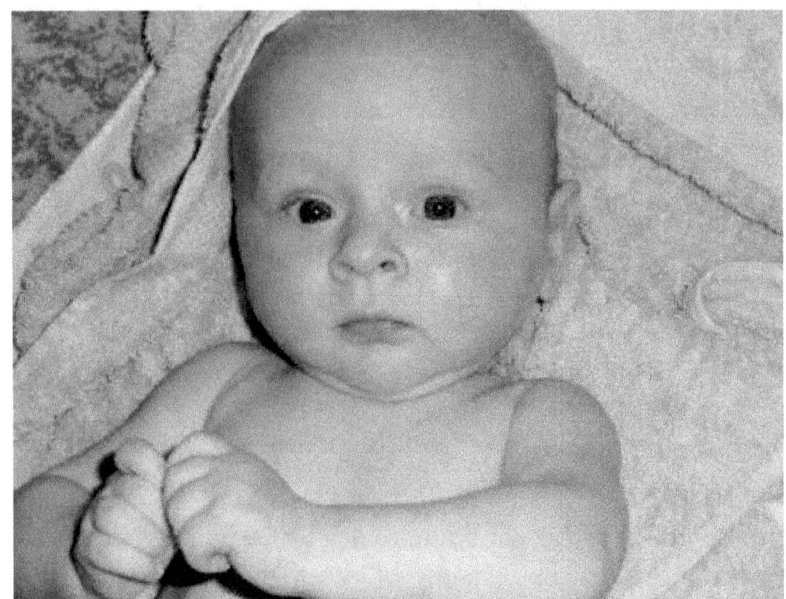

One of my all time favourite photos of Chris at 4 months old, June, 2008

Chris and Dad getting firewood for the family circa. 2009

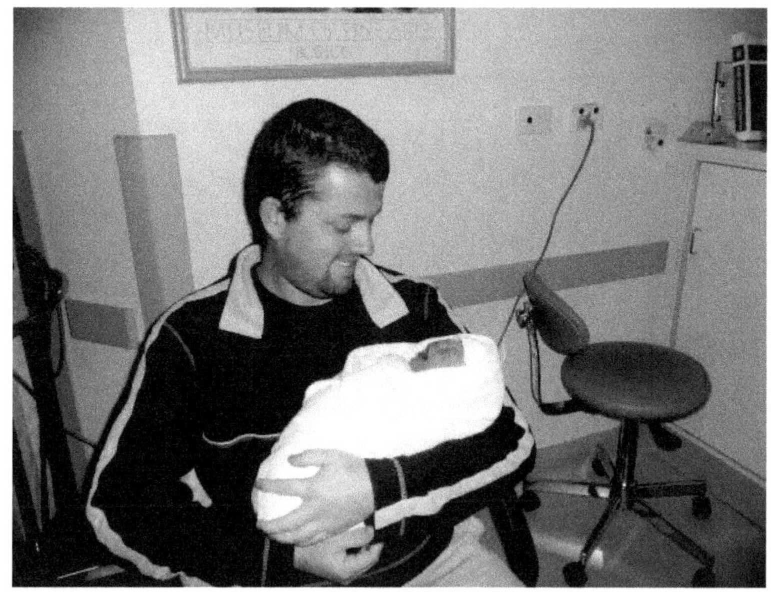

Lyndon holding his beautiful daughter Mia moments after she was born.
3 September, 2009

Photo of our beautiful children, a pigeon pair in September, 2009

CHAPTER 6

THE TIME OF OUR LIVES

"Life itself is a privilege, but to live life to the fullest - well, that is a choice"

– ANDY ANDREWS

Andy Andrews said it ever so perfectly, and that, my friends, was a choice that Lyndon and I both decided to run with. We had so many good times, both before and after our children. We really were just made for each other, and our love was so strong all those years later, just as it was when we first started dating.

Every couple, I'm sure, has their own little sayings and this was ours. We both knew, if we said this, the other was being 100% serious, no matter what. "**On our relationship**." We'd always say it, and we knew just how much we meant to each other when we used that term. We both tried to be sneaky every now and then and tried to use that term to get secrets out of each other. By secrets, I don't mean anything hidden from each other because we never did, but more so like Christmas gifts, etc, and we both could not help but tell each other what we had gotten. It's difficult to explain how much those three words meant to us as a couple, but it was extraordinary. People often said they looked up to us for relationship goals and advice. That was so heartwarming to hear that even as a couple, we were potentially helping people and sometimes didn't even know it.

Mum had moved to the United States of America when I was just 16. She was hesitant about moving to another country while I was that young, but I was already living with Lyndon, and she knew that I would be okay. When she asked me how I felt about her moving, I couldn't be happier for her. She was living her life, and I certainly was not going to be held accountable for standing in the way of that. During the separation, Facetime was a lifesaver and we regularly saw each other over the internet and as a result, she really did not feel so far away.

So, in 2004 from memory, we had our first international holiday to the USA to visit my mother. We flew over and had New Year's in the sky; it was a great experience. A different kind of experience as, yes, we were sitting in a seat, but it was just fun to know we were travelling overseas.

With -24°F/-31C° temperatures in Michigan (yes, you read that correctly), we went snowmobiling, ice fishing like you see on television, and, obviously, shopping galore. It was a holiday not to be forgotten with many great experiences and memories.

Mum took us sightseeing, as you do, to this lovely place called Tahquamenon Falls. It was a state park/forest situated in Michigan, and I remember it was absolutely breathtaking, just like the pictures. All layered up, we braved the cold to hike this beautiful area - Mum, Lyndon, and I. We were walking through the pathways and even lay on the side in the snow to experience the making of a snow angel. It started to get colder, so we were making our way back to the car when I felt a very strange sensation, as I was breathing in and out, it felt like I had a "bottle brush" going in and out of my nose. Lo and behold, my nose hairs had frozen. Laughing it off, we got back to the car, pumped the heater up, and away we drove. Now remember, Mum was an Aussie too, so she hadn't been over there all her life to know all the right things to do. When she was telling her colleagues what we did, they carefully informed her that it's actually quite dangerous and we could have very easily gotten hypothermia. The snow angel was worth it, though!

Sometime during that visit, I remember walking through a bottle shop with my mother and I was holding a bottle of alcohol. The shop attendant was abrupt when talking to my mum, because I was only 19, illegal in the United States, so he wouldn't even look at me, and I had to pass it back to Mum. I really did feel like a child. Quite comical after the event, but at the time, I was taken aback at the rudeness of the young man. I mean, I get it, I was a minor in their country, but it was completely harmless, as back here in our country, I was of legal age.

When the kidlets were 2 and 4, we took the children on their first international holiday to visit my mother, and that was another incredible experience. This time, however, we went in the summertime. The kids were witnessing a very different way of life, albeit probably too young to remember. We visited the local zoo, and afterwards, we were driving on the freeway right underneath a forming tornado. Which is quite scary looking back at it now. When we got back to Mum's house, the sirens in the street were going off, advising everyone to bunker down. We had to go into the basement underground until the sirens stopped. All houses had an underground basement. Very different from Australian houses. Truly an experience, both terrifying and thrilling. At this stage, Mia was still having day naps of 3 hours. Well, when coming home, the jetlag made damn sure that she snapped out of that and never had a day's sleep again in excess of 1 hour.

In 2015, when Chris was 7 and Mia was 6, we planned and built our forever home. We chose a beautiful parcel of land situated in Springdale Heights, called Ettamogah Rise Estate, about a 5-minute drive from our old place in Thurgoona. We sold our family home in Thurgoona in record time and moved into a rental house whilst we were in the building phase. From memory, we were only the second household to move into the area that had very little development at the time. Now, it is a major growth area and very well established. It was only a 2-minute drive from Lyndon's work and 10 minutes from mine, so all in all, it was a fantastic opportunity in an area that we both loved. The building process went smoothly enough, and even though the time felt like it dragged, we were finally able to move in.

I said, this was our perfect forever family home. This was where our family man and I were going to raise our kids and retire. Lyndon had built a big shed up the back of our block where he would tinker away doing whatever project he had going on at the time. He was extremely hands-on and meticulous with everything he did, and rarely would you find him inside, even on a rainy day.

We had one of the best front lawns on the street (if I do say so myself), with not a bindi or a weed in sight. The backyard was still a work in progress but coming along rather nicely. He loved pottering around outside and was an avid gardener, while on the other hand, I was very much a brown thumb and could kill any plant without even trying. We were a perfect yin and yang in everything we did. Even after all these years, we were rarely apart and absolutely thrived in the company of one another. We loved each other, and we loved hard. The more time that went past, the more we knew that we were made for each other. Not only were we made for each other from a couple standpoint, but now we had a young family and life was bloody perfect.

The kids slowly met all the neighbours as we were settling into our new abode, including those to the right of us and across the road from us. All the kids were around the same age, which was fantastic, and they all became pretty good mates. The kids ranged from about 6 to about 10 years old. Back in those days, the kids would hang out playing on the trampoline, swimming in the neighbours pool, riding bikes and just hanging out. A far cry from the times today where it's mainly computer games, or watching movies on Netflix, or using a mobile device.

We had really gotten into four wheel driving (4WD'ing) and loved going out any chance we got as a family. I guess looking back, that was the grown-up thing to do, as Lyndon had been through the Holden stage (remember he even had a Holden tattoo) and owned a V8, which he still cherished until he sold it to buy a 4WD to fit the kids in. We'd go up into the Victorian High Country, and because this was only a couple of hours from our front door, we'd be back in time to do our nightly routine with the kids. Those memories are ones I will value forever because we were doing exciting things as a family and cherished every moment.

We also loved camping and did this as often as we could. Our very last camping holiday as a family was at Pigs Point Reserve in Victoria. It is about an hour from Albury, and I remember picking the kids up from school. Lyndon was already out there setting up with his parents, Nan and Pop, and we drove straight out to begin our weekend. The kids still recall me being pulled over by the police on the way there because I was accidentally, maybe slightly speeding. The kids even still remember the officer's name, which I won't mention here. I am ever so grateful we got this last family camping event in, before our lives were all completely turned upside down.

I ran a successful bookkeeping and virtual administration (VA) business for many years. A virtual administrator provides remote/offsite administration services to businesses all over Australia. And my business was getting larger year by year. I worked from the comfort of our own home and was fortunate enough to work around my children when they were younger, but it did grow into a career of all hours. That was the downside of working from home, but it ultimately worked for our young family, and I had the flexibility of being my own boss, and I loved all my clients. I was extremely passionate when it came to my work, which I think is why it was so successful. You see, because Lyndon was a shift worker, I would work around him and the kids, so it wasn't unusual to find me working when the kids went off to bed and Lyndon was at work. One thing when working from home is that it can be extremely alienating. But there were online networks of other VA's all over the world, where we could connect, share ideas and talk to other people in the same boat. I still talked on the phone to clients, etc, so it wasn't all bad and quite satisfying. I loved it.

Fishing was another hobby of Lyndon's and I enjoyed it too. I thought it was quite relaxing, if the fish were biting; otherwise, I would get rather impatient. Reminiscing of the times of us going out fishing at the local Hume Weir, either on the bank or out on the boat, is a beautiful feeling as I can still remember his big beaming smile. I remember when I wasn't long out of the hospital after my stroke and on some pretty strong blood thinners, Lyndon had arranged a day on the water, just fishing and relaxing. Coming back in for the day, I was getting out of the boat (or at least, I was attempting to), and I slipped ever so lightly. That evening, I noticed my thigh was absolutely black and blue. I realised how careful I needed to be now as that bump was so minor, yet the bruise covered a decent chunk of my thigh.

The week before Lyndon's workplace incident, he said he wanted to start training Chris in ten-pin bowling. I could see the special look on his face when he spoke about it. He lit up. He was going to start training his only son. Of course, I was over the moon and welcomed the idea. It is hard to believe we only ever got to the talking stage with this, as his son is exactly like him when it comes to bowling. Bowling for us is more than a social sport; it is ingrained in our family.

Little did we know the cards that would be dealt next. One piece of advice that I urge everyone reading this to take is to create unlimited memories, always. Bucket List, anyone?

I have learnt through all of this that memories are what count the most! Bucket Lists for me hold a whole new meaning. It means living life in the "now." Living a life with no regrets and chasing your dreams no matter how big or small. Since knowing this, we have created the Quinny Bucket List. And we regularly make additions to this list. Why? Because we have experienced firsthand, not once but twice, how short our time here on this earth is. I want our children to remember the good times, the happy times, and the positive times.

In the last 2 years, we have been on 2 cruises (yes, I am hooked) with one of those being to the all-amazing New Zealand. That was absolutely exhilarating, and I loved every single second of it. Chris wants to go to Malaysia for the Milo (ten-pin bowling) tournament, and we certainly will do that. For us, it's just about doing stuff that WE want to create a lasting memory. I urge everyone reading this to please do the same: Create those memories.

Some of the things we have done since 2018:

- 2 Cruises (one to an overseas destination – New Zealand)
- Chris and Mia have each gotten tattoo's in memory of their father.
- Chris won his father's bowling tournament.
- Moved states from NSW to QLD.
- I have got a new car and joined the Lexus club.
- Fulfilled my personal milestone of writing this book, which Lyndon was in support of back when I had my stroke.

A MOMENT OF REFLECTION

I know just how important creating memories is. The importance of this was compounded when Lyndon was tragically taken from us, far too soon, from an incident that was, indeed, 100% preventable.

REFLECTION QUESTIONS:

1. Have you got a bucket list? If so, how much of it is crossed off (completed)?
   If not, I urge you to create a "family bucket list" (and a personal one too, if that's what you would like) and make a conscious effort to regularly tick off items. Place it somewhere central, like on your fridge, where it will always be in the forefront of your mind.

2. You do not need money to do everything. If you need to start out small because of financial issues, creating memories during family outings at the park, or camping will have the same effect. Trust me!

3. Take a LOT of family photos to capture memories. Ensure to have EVERYONE in there. All too often, obviously, me included, one person is the photographer, so all family photos are always one less family member. I don't ever want to make this mistake again. Because when you're gone, these memories become extremely important to surviving members.

A picture of Mia, Mum & Dad taken when she was approx 4 months old

Chris bowling at 3D Lanes in Wodonga. A spitting image of his father, circa. 2022

Chris & Dad - Loving the boys will be boys vibe

Chris & Mia - Sibling Love

Chris at Sunset Superbowl in Toowoomba, 2021. The same stance that his dad had in Wodonga

Dad & Chris - Watching the car races together, circa. 2011

Family trip to USA, 2012

Jacci (Mum) & Mia at a lakeside wedding, 2010

Lyndon & Jacci, 2018. One of my favourite photos

Lyndon at 3D Lanes in Wodonga - Same bowling style as his son approx 2015

Lyndon (Dad) and his girl, Mia, 2010. Loves her daddy so much

Lyndon at 3D Lanes in Wodonga. Like father like son. circa. 2016

Lyndon's cheeky smile, 2018

Mia & Dad having an awesome time at the park, 2017

Our last family photo, 2017

CHAPTER 7

A PREVENTABLE WORKPLACE INCIDENT

"Safety is not an intellectual exercise to keep us in work. It is a matter of life and death. It is the sum of our contributions to safety management that determines whether the people we work with live or die"

– SIR BRIAN APPLETON

First and foremost, I feel the need to take this opportunity to echo the **Trigger Warning** written at the beginning of the book before you advance through this chapter.

May 23, 2018, a Wednesday much like all the others. The kids were now 10 and 8 years old. Looking back now, it was a day filled with "lasts" for our family, marking a significant moment of reflection amongst catastrophic and unexpected circumstances. It is that evening that I think about the most. It was our last beautiful, family dinner that we had. We always had dinner at the table to instill that all-imperative family time into our young, growing children. Lyndon loved experimenting in the kitchen and he assisted with dinner that night. It was the very last goodnight kiss he planted on his children's foreheads as they drifted off into their slumber. Recalling the last time we spent as a couple, as we always did, we were together, cuddling on the couch and watching our favourite TV series, The Big Bang Theory as well as MythBusters (Lyndon was rather scientific and had to know how certain things worked.) I have not been able to bring myself to watch these shows again since. Nestling up against him whilst we slept is something I will never ever forget. He embraced me ever so tight as he always did. Lyndon loved me so much, and this never went unnoticed. I was truly fortunate to have a doting husband like him. That evening, we both drifted off to sleep, in each other's arms, totally unaware these were our final moments together, never to be had again.

The 24th of May 2018, had started off as an ordinary day in our residence. Lyndon planted a kiss on my forehead as I was still half asleep, then he snuck into the kids rooms to give them a goodbye kiss, as was his daily routine. He proceeded on his way to work for a typical day shift. This day was a scheduled 3-day maintenance, a "shut" as they called it. A day when they had to do repairs, maintenance, and/or cleaning. They regularly did these types of shuts, and he had worked there for many years, so there really were no issues or concerns that either of us had. Just another regular, expected day at the worksite.

I began my morning routine of getting myself ready for work and getting the kids dressed and ready for school. I dropped them off at the bus stop, which was not far from our house, and made my way to work. At this time in our lives, I was working as a Self-Managed Superannuation Fund (SMSF) Administration Manager with a local accounting firm. Things were beginning to pick up steadily, we were busy with the end of the financial year (EOFY) very quickly creeping up on us. I was lucky because I absolutely loved my job and worked with amazing people for whom I am forever grateful.

I was in a work meeting just after midday when a call had come in for me. I instantly knew that something was off when our meeting had to be interrupted for me to take this call. I asked if I could call whoever it was back. It was in this very moment that my world started to collapse around me. I was told that I had to take this call, and making matters worse, it was from Lyndon's dad, my father-in-law. I can still hear his voice on the other end of that phone, just like a chilling telephone recording on replay, telling me to pack up my stuff and make my way to Lyndon's place of work. I asked if Lyndon was okay and the words "we'll see" was all he could say.

My work colleague and friend (bless her) insisted she drive me to his place of work, as it was by now, unmistakable that I was in no shape to drive. Approximately 20 minutes or so later, we arrived, and I was met at the front gate by Lyndon's father. He took my arm and we went into the administration building and straight upstairs into a large boardroom which overlooked the car park. When I think of this, I still don't remember my feet touching the ground; all I remember is his dad taking my hand. It was truly an out-of-body experience, and the next thing I knew, my twinkle toes had me upstairs in that room. I can also still replay this memory like a video on repeat. After all the years of Lyndon working there, this was the very first time I had ever set foot past those entry gates. The first and the last time, as there is no way I could ever return to that place knowing what had transpired.

It was in those moments when I was told that Lyndon, another colleague and a further contractor, who I'm led to believe was a newish contractor at the worksite, had all been overcome by extremely toxic levels of the deadly Hydrogen Sulphide (H2S) gas. This gas is also commonly known as rotten egg gas or sour gas. Yes, three people at the one time. Despite the following days, and even weeks, of extreme busyness, I can recall every slight and even miniscule detail.

At this stage, we did not know any further information because the situation was rapidly unfolding and changing. A short while later, someone came into the boardroom, where my father-in-law and I were, asking me if I wanted a tea or coffee. I am sure this was very uncomfortable for this gentleman and he was just doing the polite thing. Lyndon must have painted a very nice picture of me, as everyone knew I would never turn down a cup of tea – or so we'd thought. Understandably, I replied to his question with "No! I want to know how my husband is?"

We were then told that the paramedics were trying everything they could to get Lyndon's heart working. This really was a nightmare, like I was in a horror movie! What was I hearing right now? He was completely fine when he left for work this morning, I recall thinking to myself, trying to process everything I was listening to.

The same gentleman came in a short time later and said something along the lines of, "They have his heart working and he's now in the ambulance being taken to our local hospital."

Hearing those words at this time, I just remember a great sense of relief wash over me. If his heart was working, my thought was he was going to be okay! Little did I know how very wrong I was. I was dead-set certain that everything from this point forward would be okay. I mean, I knew this incident was extremely serious, don't get me wrong when I say that. But his heart was working and now we can just deal with getting him better, together, as a family. That was my thought.

By now, my mother-in-law had just arrived at the worksite. We were able to see her coming as we were watching out of the upstairs boardroom window. My father-in-law took me by the hand and again my twinkle toes had me out to the car park before I knew it, where I was placed in her car and told to go directly to the hospital. We were now en-route to the hospital and I recall thinking about my kids. I had to somehow organise the children's school pickup without even knowing what the hell was going on.

I quickly phoned a friend and asked him to collect our kids from school and take them back to his house. At that point in time, I did not foresee that we would be at the hospital so long – I mean, his heart was working, remember? He was going to be okay. Hindsight is always a good thing and the denial alarm bells were loudly chiming away this day.

We were not fully aware at this time, but would eventually find out that multiple workplace failures led to the catastrophic injuries that would very soon take the lives of both Lyndon's colleague (a beautiful, lively, and active young man with his whole life ahead of him) and Lyndon (forever our family man and our hero.) This disastrous event additionally led to the contractor being placed in an induced coma and, subsequently, making a full recovery.

We had just pulled into the hospital car park after what felt like the longest drive known to mankind. It was like a scene from the movies with all the ambulances and I think there were also fire engines and police cars. There was an ambulance parked at the front entrance of the emergency department with the back doors wide open. I could see a pair of lifeless legs on the stretcher bed in the back, which I was sure was my husband's. Instantly, I started making a beeline for it. However, as quickly as I approached the ambulance, I was just as swiftly cut off by the paramedic and told to go the other way. I completely understand they were just doing their job, and they didn't know who I was, but this time, their job involved the care of our world, our family man!

We hurried into the emergency department, marching straight up to the triage/emergency counter, where I said my husband had been brought in from an incident at work. They were ready and waiting for us to arrive and we were immediately escorted into a very small room. My in-laws were with me, including my sister-in-law, who was heavily pregnant at the time. I will never know how the stress of what had just unfolded and what was still to happen didn't send her into early labour. All I know is that I am ever so grateful we were all there for one another as a family unit, just as Lyndon would want.

At some stage later in the afternoon, I had a brief moment while waiting in the room to phone and update my mother, who was now living in South East Queensland. She was still at work when I told her there had been an incident in which Lyndon was involved. I proceeded to say he's currently in the hospital, but that's all they are telling us. I hung up feeling completely helpless as I had no further information to share with her. My father-in-law had to be taken back into the Emergency department for checking as he was also working at the site and was affected by the poisonous gas, along with numerous members of his crew who were in emergency at this time. By the time he was given the green light to return to his family, he walked back to the very small room where we were waiting, his head down. All he could muster up to say was that Lyndon's colleague was gone. That moment was so strange and surreal. To this day, I still cannot explain the feeling that was running through me. Every step of this was a living nightmare.

The doctors and nurses came in numerous times to check how we were. However, each time they couldn't give us any new information other than they're "still working on him." Again, the doctor came in, I think about 5 hours later, which to us obviously felt like a bloody lifetime, and said Lyndon was very sick. Again, the amazing thing that hindsight is, I know now the doctor was trying to prepare us.

However, I was still in a state of denial and I couldn't let those words sink in. I was completely adamant that Lyndon would be okay. I still had hope. He was alive! This was our Lyndon. Nothing like this happens to him. We just had to deal with getting him better as a family, just as we always did. Just as we did when my stroke occurred all those years earlier. I was clutching at straws by this stage and I am sure this was beginning to wear very thin on the doctor. We said our vows of sickness and health, and I was adamant I was going to see that through.

I am sure the medical fraternity deals with people just like me, in total shock, every day, but I felt (at the time) certain they were getting increasingly frustrated that I was not comprehending the seriousness of this situation. I now know it was not sinking in, but at the time, I was in a state of disbelief, numbness, and pure devastation, as were my in-laws. This is not something anybody can ever imagine until you're living through it.

Numerous cardiac arrests later, we could finally go and sit with him. That was one of the most confronting things I have ever witnessed in my life. My normally bubbly, fun-loving, and jovial husband was lying completely lifeless with tubes, monitors, and wires all over the place. As the workers were exposed to such high toxic levels of this deadly rotten egg gas (H2S), everything had to be destroyed. His clothes, work boots, all clothing that was on him, that was, except his jocks. Why just his jocks, you may be wondering? He was so unstable that every time they tried to cut his jocks off, we were told it would throw him into another cardiac arrest. I just sat by his head, holding his hand, not even able to kiss his forehead since all of the tubes and monitors were in the way. I recall, I just interlocked his hand with mine, hoping he would wake up, wishing I would wake up from this unbearable dream.

I recall rubbing his head ever so softly, and then I felt a little lump. Upon closer examination, there was a petite mole, so naturally, I requested the nurse to take a look at it. I think the lovely nurse at the time knew I was clutching at straws and just said something along the lines of "I'll note it in his chart, and we'll take a look once he's better." Looking back, I believe she knew Lyndon was not coming out of this. Again, I still had hope, remember. This kind of thing does not happen to Lyndon. And I was fully prepared, willing, and able to nurse him back to health, in whatever way, shape, or form that may have looked like. We truly honoured those vows of "in sickness and in health" that we had made all those years earlier.

In the very early hours of the following morning, the doctor had asked us to step outside to speak to us. We were asked to make the decision that nobody should ever have to make - to turn off his life support. Being his wife, that decision ultimately fell on me. His mother was beside me nodding her head giving me her approval. From a mother's perspective, can you imagine the pain that she must have been going through - a premature loss of the life of your child, going before you. And he was only 35 years old – completely healthy and absolutely loving life! There is nothing in the so-called parenting manual about having to bury your own child. Yet, she was trying to remain strong for us!

Moments before they switched off his life support, we found ourselves saying our goodbyes. I remember clearly kissing his forehead and saying to him that I will take care of our children and I will make him damn proud of both his children and me, his wife. I promised him that I would never stop fighting for change, justice, and accountability. Little did I know at the time, I had just conceived my life's mission and purpose. And I will continue to uphold my promise to my very last breath.

As I write this, I can feel the lump in my throat and tears welling in my eyes. The loss of a husband and best friend cannot be explained and accompanies you forever. I have come to realise that I carry this longing and ache in my heart, and will until the day I die. I believe this is the price for loving so deeply. I believe we were dealt the ultimate sentence for a crime we did not commit.

Please do not judge here because this next one may stir a few pots, but to "forgive" for this level of incident is simply not in my capacity. That is something I just cannot see myself doing. However, I will choose to make peace (one day at a time) for myself, for my kids, and lastly for our family man. I am choosing to be able to move forward with Lyndon in our lives, which I know is what he would ultimately want for us.

This incident resulted in three individuals whose lives were changed forever. Two of which were abruptly and prematurely taken. Then, another colleague and very good workmate felt so guilty and responsible that he felt the only way out was by taking his own life (which you will read about in a later chapter.) You read that right. A colleague dying by suicide in response to this tragedy was thrown into the mix. Now, we were dealing with 3 lives taken far too soon and a 4th forever altered. Then, the ripple effects for the families of the deceased is that we are the ones who are dealt a life sentence. We are living our lives without the person who is supposed to be here. It just felt like the kicks kept coming whilst we were already knocked down and brutally beaten.

Friday, the 25th of May 2018, is now a day that tortures our family. I was only 32 years old, and now I was rendered a "widow" with 2 small children. I had been with Lyndon since I was 15 years old. I shouldn't have had to make that decision to end his life. No one should. I should have been given the opportunity to nurse him back to health, just as he did me when I suffered my stroke. Instead, that right was stolen from us.

When the judge handed down the sentence, the proceedings found a number of failures by the employer company. As an employee in Australia and under WHS laws, he and his colleagues had a right to a safe and a healthy workplace. I firmly believe a part of this is to return home to their family safely after their shift has ended and, certainly in this instance, this did not happen.

Everything was such a blur, so I hadn't had a chance to update Mum in the hospital that night. And I couldn't think straight after he passed. I was in a state of total shock. Little did I know that at about 6am that Friday morning, my mother was already on her way down to us on a flight. She had landed in Sydney and phoned to see what was happening and how Lyndon was and all I could say was "He's gone."

She absolutely lost it, yet still had to board a much smaller flight from Sydney to ultimately reach us. I remember her saying on the flight, there were 2 women sitting in the row in front of her speaking about what unfolded yesterday and that 2 men had perished. All she could do was look out the window, but what she really wanted was to yell at them to please just be quiet. She landed at the local airport at about 9am, from memory, and a good friend had arranged to pick her up and bring her to my in-laws' place, which is where we all were. As soon as I saw her, I collapsed into her arms and we just wept.

That day, after turning off his life support, a piece of me died with my husband. I have been asked if the "old" me will ever return, and although I understand the innocence in the question itself, the answer is a big, fat NO. Those 2 days forever changed me, and I morphed into a completely different person. Some would say an unrecognisable person. After an experience like that, you can't help but change. The rug had been pulled from underneath me and my family. How could anything possibly ever be the same again unless some kind of miracle happened and this turned out to all be a bad dream, which we knew now would not happen. This was not a dream but a living, bloody nightmare.

We were not completely aware at the time, but this incident was waiting to transpire. How? Because on this fateful day, liquid was witnessed running down the side of a tank which had, not 1, but 2 splits in it. There was hardened, built-up pulp residue around the edges of the splits, indicating the damage was not new. We later found out that the liquid appeared to be filtrate. Lyndon's colleague was the first to go up as he was asked to see what was going on. Naturally, he climbed a fixed ladder on the side of the tank, but what was up top was not enough room to even stand up, and he was rendered unconscious.

A good mate of the workers and colleague, who was a part of the furniture at the worksite, climbed up the ladder, felt lightheaded, and just assumed he'd overexerted himself (he was back on his first shift and on light duties following surgery.) He immediately climbed down and radioed to the control room, where my husband was, and said "man down," to which Lyndon immediately ran out, as he was the 1st-aider, and took the contractor with him. They both climbed up the attached ladder, first Lyndon and then the contractor. Again, I heard they were rendered unconscious almost immediately. Lyndon's father, at this stage, had to be held back from attempting to go up to save his son and the other men. The tank where this incident occurred was approximately 5 metres high. It was also found to be in a poor state at the time of the incident and that no-one had inspected or assessed the tank for a long time, according to the court documents.

The court proceedings found that from the lip of the tank top to the underside of the concrete floor above had a variance of 1.3 metres to 1.5 metres. My first thought, and I wasn't even a person with a safety background, was this not a confined space if you can't stand up?

A lot of us have heard of the term but what is a confined space? According to a SafeWork NSW publication, a confined space is by definition a space that is enclosed or partially enclosed that is not designed for human occupation. It is meant to be at normal atmospheric pressure while any human is in that space and or it is likely to be a risk to their health and safety. In this specific case, the judge's findings stated that the likelihood of the risk occurring was quite high and the employer company had failed to designate the space above the top of the tank as a confined space or restricted area. This was just one of the failings listed when the sentence was handed down.

A MOMENT OF REFLECTION

I said this was raw, and no matter the time that passes, this is still so difficult to write. On the same token, no matter how difficult this is for me, I am determined to make people aware so that something so tragic does not happen again.

REFLECTION QUESTIONS:

1. One of the most difficult things I have had to come to terms with is the feeling that I turned off his life support so soon, perhaps prematurely. I was only 32 and this was the medical recommendation at the time. But a part of me still feels responsible, as the decision fell on me as his wife. I now know I haven't processed this properly and still blame myself, but I am working through this. For anyone going through this type of guilt, please get help from a professional.

2. What have you been holding onto that you feel you need to let go of? How will you do that? Do you think you will feel a bit lighter?

3. If you are not ready to let someone go (if you are their next of kin), then DON'T.
   Do it in your own time.

4. I wish I had thought to get a lock of his hair, a cast of our hands, a photo as a "last" of us. It is a regret, and I can't do anything about it now. It may sound morbid to some, but it's not. I know people who got a cast of the mother's hands interlocking the child. I've known people to get a lock of hair or even a fingerprint for keepsake jewellery. My point is, you will never be able to get this chance again, and for me, I wish I had. You ARE able to ask for this, and I recommend that you do. Have a think about what would hold the most meaning for you.

Lyndon - His beautiful soft smile prior to our worlds forever changing

CHAPTER 8

ADVERSITY HIT AGAIN, EVEN HARDER

"It's through adversity that you find the strength you never knew you had."

– CHRISTIE BRINKLEY

Perhaps I did not learn the first time we were struck down? Opinions such as this are certainly what had crossed my mind at the time, and many times subsequently. Why are we going through this? What have we ever done to deserve this? Did we kill a black cat? My mind was anything but still, as you could probably appreciate.

I can't remember when it was, but I think a mere few days after, I had a call from someone at the Coroner's office to say that Lyndon was being taken by road for an autopsy. My heart just sank even further. Nobody in the hospital had mentioned that he needed to be sent for an autopsy, not that I can recall anyway, and I had not the faintest clue leading up to it. Why did they not inform us BEFORE now, I kept thinking? I was furious. If it could be seen, there would have been steam coming out of my ears. I was angry. I was scared. I should have been with him to advocate for him. I remember feeling the sensation of terror and fear rush over me because Lyndon was in the back of a van for the 6 or so hour trip along the Highway all alone. I remember feeling how scared he must have been. I knew he had passed but I hadn't accepted it yet. Even though he was dead, I still wanted him treated like he was still alive. Perhaps that was a part of the processing in my brain. How much more did he need to endure? Hadn't he been through enough already?

I remember asking them to call me as soon as they arrived in Newcastle. How silly I must have sounded to them, but at the end of the day, they were simply transporting a deceased body. Whereas for me, it was personal. They had precious cargo, our family man!

They called me and notified me of his arrival, and to be honest, the lady on the other end of that phone was lovely and somewhat reassuring, given the difficult task of speaking to bereaved and grieving families who were still in a state of shock and disbelief. They mentioned the things they would be doing as part of the autopsy and went through everything meticulously. They mentioned having to potentially slice him open, and this naturally scared me even more. The damaging thoughts of them cutting open his body in my mind were having a field day. I pleaded with them not to do it unless absolutely necessary, even though I knew they would do it anyway if there was a particular need. A day or two later, they called me on the phone and informed me they had completed the autopsy and they were sending him back to our hometown. Naturally, he was returning to the funeral home, and I asked for a call the moment he arrived back at the funeral home.

By this time, we had to start the funeral preparations for a couple of weeks later, as this was also to allow time for the autopsy, so it was decided the service would be on the 6th June, 2018. I made damn sure my in-laws accompanied me to the church while my mum stayed at home with the kids. Lyndon and I and his parents were a close-knit family and they brought him into this world. There was no way in hell I was excluding them from these important decisions. They are his parents and they are my parents too. The love and support they have always shown us and our kids, and continue to do so to this day, are what I will always cherish. I love them more than words can describe. I am forever indebted to them and grateful to call them my family. An event such as this quite often rips families apart and I have heard so many horror stories. But at the end of the day, I personally knew how much "family" had meant to us all and this certainly was not going to undo that.

The other young man's family held his funeral. We hadn't met yet, but I remember speaking to this gentleman's mother, and due to the very public nature of both funerals, we chose not to attend the funeral for him out of respect and his family did the same for Lyndon. We mutually agreed that both men needed to have their own farewell days. From what I saw, he had a beautiful service with a guard of honour just like Lyndon did. All the employees from his work attended the funeral in their full work attire out of respect.

The dreaded day rolled around quickly, and I honestly don't remember Lyndon's service much at all. I remember just trying to keep it together for the children's sake. We clearly sat in the front row and the church was absolutely jam-packed. I kind of remember planning the funeral, from the songs to the photos, selecting the men who carried out his coffin, but it was a real blur. I think it was a coping mechanism and the fact that I can't remember too much now, I'd actually go so far as to say it still is. I do hope that I remember more as my body and brain process things.

Just before Lyndon's funeral, I remember a colleague of the boys at work, not to mention a good mate of both, was feeling extremely responsible. He had asked the first man to go up and investigate and was of the opinion that it was his fault the boys were now dead. I asked my father-in-law to get him over so I could tell him that Lyndon and I did not blame him in any way and it was NOT his fault. He came over and Lyndon's father disappeared to Lyndon's shed for privacy so we could both talk and mourn together.

He was absolutely riddled with guilt. I could see that, but I also felt that he had accepted the fact that we did not hold him responsible as we believed it was the failures of the company. We were sitting on my couch. He hugged me ever so tightly, and we just stayed in that embrace for what felt like a very, very long time. What I did not realise at the time (hindsight is always a valuable lesson) was that it was his way of saying goodbye to me. The day after Lyndon's funeral, I had yet another call to let us know that some representatives of Lyndon's work needed to speak to us in person. I phoned Lyndon's parents and asked them to come straight over as we were about to receive some more news.

At about 8pm, from memory, they had to tell us this colleague had taken his own life earlier that day. Tragedy and sadness seemed to be everywhere and knowing that this good friend of Lyndon and his colleagues would not be returning home was so excruciatingly sad.

Let me be 100% clear, this incident, however, was not his fault at all. In a time such as this, when the workers are all so close as it is, and most have witnessed such a catastrophic event, making sure their own mental health is catered to is absolutely paramount.

All three funerals were held at the same location. We were advised of this location due to the size of the church and the expected turnout as it rocked the whole community. Again, I have never been able to walk through those church gates since. I know I say 'never say never.'

However, on this occasion, I really cannot see myself going back to these locations.

After the hurricane that was Lyndon's funeral, I opted to have him cremated and to be laid to rest in our hometown in NSW. When I got the phone call to say he was ready to be picked up, I think I was there within about 15 minutes to collect and bring home my husband. What a feeling that was, too awful for words. Here I was, a 32 year old widow arriving to collect her husband in a small box. Carefully placing him in the car, I ensured that I wrapped the seatbelt around him firmly. On my arrival at home, he was without delay put on our vanity benchtop in our ensuite, which overlooked our bedroom. For some reason, I felt that Lyndon was home where he belonged, and I felt somewhat safe again?! It may sound silly, but I had him with us again.

I remember that evening, I heard something and got out of bed to see where the noise had come from. Our ensuite overlooked our entire bedroom with a big mirror from wall to wall. As I stood up, I remember absolutely shitting myself thinking someone was in our room. Perhaps it was Lyndon? Naturally, that was my first thought running around my overthinking brain but, instead, it was my very own shadow in the darkness of the mirror. I can smile about that now.

Choosing what to do with his ashes was yet another decision altogether. To be honest, I wanted to keep him home on my vanity where he could look over me and always keep me safe. I did think about getting a ring made from his ashes, but I knew it was not just me I had to think about. I had to take my in-laws into consideration, and of course, our children. They all needed the ability to be able to go somewhere too. So I decided to look for a special plot out at the local crematorium. I asked my mother-in-law to accompany me as again this was a big decision. I felt it only right to have her input. I remember we got out there and got in this golf buggy and drove around the crematorium for a while with the lady who manages it and saw a few potential spots. They were all nice but none were jumping out.

Then, when we came across the spot where he is laid to rest now, I just knew that Lyndon would appreciate this outlook for many reasons. His new, final forever home was overlooking the hills and right behind it was a bench seat, so it just made sense. We chose there and I selected a Little Gem Magnolia as the tree because Lyndon loved his plants and was definitely a green thumb. (If you can remember, I was the brown thumb when it came to plants.) That's when the magnolia for me became the link to Lyndon. His mother and I selected his plaque and chose what words to put on there. It's beautiful and it really encapsulates him as the family man he was. I know he would approve of all the heartbreaking decisions I had to make, time and time again.

Not only were we now dealing with the massive gaping hole of his absence, but we were also tossed into a legal battlefield and minefield, dealing with the investigating bodies and also a multitude of other entities that nobody is aware of until you go through it yourself. I was dealing with numerous solicitors, as we needed separate ones for me and for my children. Then there were the insurance companies, superannuation, the media, police, state coroner, funeral home, and the list went on. All of these companies had specific jobs to do and I understand that. However, the main theme I felt was how impersonal the dealings usually were. At the end of the day, my feelings were that companies such as these close their files and computers and completely switch off until the next day. But for us, it was always there, 24/7. So many people have a misconception about what you need to endure when dealing with a workplace fatality and, I will admit, I certainly did not know what went on. I guess for people who aren't dealing with this directly, you can take it as a learning outcome to really understand the complexities surrounding such deaths and, in turn, be more compassionate to those who are in the thick of it.

You are totally unprepared to travel this path and, really, can't be. It's not going to all be complete in a few short months like many believe. In my situation, approximately 2 years after his death, the investigation found enough evidence to move forward with a prosecution. That was just the decision to prosecute. Now they still need to follow the steps to get there - paperwork, setting court dates, and multiple court mentions. It is anything but a quick process. What I will tell you from my personal experience, and almost everyone I have spoken to about this has said the same thing, is that during this time not much at all is disclosed to you. You feel you are treated almost as if you are the one that was in the wrong to start with. I did NOT kill my husband yet I was made to feel like the person that had. This is where, I believe, these companies and legal systems need more empathy-based training. I firmly believe that workplace legislation, policies and processes need to be brought up to speed with the current times. That is my own personal opinion.

I learnt that prosecution doesn't always go ahead even if they know a company is guilty. Again thinking about this from the point of view of the family of affected persons - What the actual hell?? They only proceed to prosecution if there is enough evidence that they are likely to win a case! That was told to me before they had decided to go ahead with the prosecution of the employer. To me, it appears it's only about looking good and winning - not anything to do with the morals of a company doing the wrong thing and holding them to account. No real justice for the men we lost at all. My pretty stern view is the system is failing. It failed Lyndon, it failed me, and it failed my family!

The date of our incident was 24/05/2018, and the handing down of the sentence or decision date was 25/09/2020. That's 2 years, 4 months, and 1 day. 856 days is apparently very quick when you are talking about an investigation in the workplace. Can you imagine the pain we endured of being in complete limbo and not knowing whether you are Arthur or Martha for that period of time?

One thing that I learnt through this process is that some dishonest companies try to, if at risk of prosecution, do something called phoenixing. Now this is illegal, and although it's very rare, it's been known to happen. And if you are going through what we were, it's almost always on the minds of the families left behind. Obviously, during the 2 plus years of investigation, I was afraid of this. In my head I thought, "They will try anything to get out of this."

Then they decided to sell the local jobsite, which sent alarm bells ringing. Perhaps it was a grieving widow symptom, but I wanted somebody to be held to account for the untimely death of my husband! The local site where the incident occurred was sold with production of the newsprint stopping in late 2019. They sold for multi-millions. Despite selling in 2019, a prosecution was still able to go ahead, which I am grateful for.

During the prosecution, the court proceedings confirmed that at the time of the incident, a siren was not working. How, in today's society of workplace health and safety, was there a siren that was not working? Was there not a safety drill that regularly happened to ensure these were in working order? Was there proper and adequate air ventilation? So many questions were running rampant through my already racing brain. These were my thoughts day in and day out. Not a day went by without these thoughts running through my head.

I must say, the judge who was on this specific case was great, all things considered. I certainly was not happy with the outcome, and I never would have been, but he was acting within the realms of what he could do by law. SafeWork won the case and the company was fined a figure of $1.35 million, but also had given them an early guilty plea discount of 25% leaving a total fine of $1,012,500! The judge had stated that he found that the company's level of culpability was in the high range. As an affected family member, put yourself in our shoes and try to link that measly fine of $1,012,000 to the value of lives. Can you understand why I believe it's a slap on the wrist and merely petty cash for the company?

Now, I don't think you will find many affected family members, like myself, who think that a 25% discount is at all fair when someone dies or is severely injured at work. However, this is written into the legislation, so the judge had to allow for this. I myself, along with many, many others, will continue to try and have laws and legislation amended as a "discount" is not okay! Where is our discount? We did no wrong! I feel the system failed Lyndon, me, our children, and his parents and sister.

The other thing here is, remember, we are not talking about only ONE fatality in this case, there were two. But this was the overall fine the company had to pay for the incident. In my opinion, as I just mentioned, it's petty cash.

Again, the judge ruled that the likelihood of the risk occurring was in fact "quite high." When the sentence was handed down, hearing the list of failures by the company on the court documents, was confronting. They failed to do simple things that would otherwise have given our men a fighting chance. Things like failing to designate a set confined space, failing to repair or simply be aware of the two splits in the tank, failing to ensure adequate ventilation, training ALL workers in confined spaces and hazardous gas risks, and of course, the failure to have provision of personal hazardous gas monitors. Back in 2018, and still in today's society, I personally would have thought that safety issues like the above-mentioned would be a no-brainer, right?

Once this prosecution was finalised, I received notification that no inquest was going ahead despite my numerous attempts for one. I was livid to hear this. I could be wrong, but from my understanding, the purpose of an inquest/inquiry is not to point blame, so to speak, but to ensure this would not happen again in the future. I honestly believed that there were so many insights to take from this specific case. Yet again, I personally feel the system completely failed the men who died and all workers everywhere. There's only so much you can deal with when going through so much already, so I conceded defeat here to a broken system.

Now, it was my civil case that I had to get underway, which was the next piece in the process. For anyone who goes down this path, again, you may hear a common theme.

I felt like I was treated as though I had done something wrong, and the level of scrutiny was overwhelming. From my perspective, it often felt as though the focus was on minimising what would be paid to me and my children.

I found the process incredibly confronting and, at times, disheartening. It left me questioning how decisions were being made and whether compassion had a place in it.

This is my personal experience, and how it felt to me. Others may see it differently, but for me, it was one of the hardest parts of the journey.

A MOMENT OF REFLECTION

Stay a family and come together to mourn together.
All too often, you hear stories about families falling apart because the person who has just passed was the glue. Please, I urge you all to have a think about what your loved one would have wanted, not what "you" need. It's hard to do sometimes, but families NEED to come together at such a time like this, not drift further apart. It's imperative to understand that everyone else grieves differently and every loss is hardest for the person going through it.

If you haven't lost anyone in such a traumatic way, the absolute worst thing you can say is "I understand." Because you don't. And, honestly, we don't want you to understand because that means yet another life would be needlessly taken.

Please talk about them, the loved ones we've lost.
The best thing to do is LISTEN and TALK ABOUT THE MEMORIES OF THEM.

People far too often shy away from that because of the fear of upsetting us, but it's the exact opposite as we want them remembered. My mother-in-law and I have grown very close during this difficult time. I can empathise with her as she can with me. However, I haven't lost a son, so I can't truly understand her loss and never will try. At the very same time, she can empathise with me for losing my husband and best friend, but she can never understand the pain that I had to endure and still endure. You can't unless you have

> physically walked in our specific shoes. I think that's why we get each other so well and we are able to talk about Lyndon openly.

REFLECTION QUESTIONS:

1. One very important factor to consider, no matter your age or gender, is what your wishes would be in the event of your untimely death. Is this something that you have considered or spoken to your spouse or your family about? If not, why not?

2. Have you decided on whether you would like to be cremated or buried? This is such a personal decision, and it's important to remember that there is NO right or wrong answer.

3. Would you like to become an organ donor in the event of your death? These are questions sometimes we don't like to think about, but it's imperative to have these decisions figured out.

In loving memory
Of a cherished husband & father
Lyndon Quinlivan
12/10/1982 – 25/05/2018
Loved and remembered, every single day.
You left us beautiful memories,
Your love is still our guide,
Although we cannot see you,
You're always by our side
Love always and forever,
Jacci, Chris & Mia XOXO

Border Mail In memorium

QUINLIVAN
Lyndon
12.10.1982 ~ 25.5.2018
We climbed trees &
dreamed big dreams together.
Though life now branches apart,
our roots forever entwined.
We are covered in the memories of you,
Love always and forever.
– Jacci, Chris & Mia xxxooo

Each year we put our memorium in the paper for his anniversary

Lyndon Funeral Service on 6 June, 2018

Lyndon's final resting place in our hometown, Albury, NSW

CHAPTER 9

FINANCIAL IMPLICATIONS

"The harder you work, the luckier you get."

– GARY PLAYER

Everyone is entitled to their own opinions, and my personal opinions are no exception to this rule. This quote above about working harder and getting luckier, well, I beg to differ with it and I'm quite firm on this. I know, based on my own experience, that it is completely untrue. I must say, however, I think the rationale behind his above quote is slightly different in context, and if it hadn't been for my experiences, I would have probably agreed. Lyndon would have agreed with this quote as well and was an exceptionally hard worker. Lyndon and I were of the belief that if we worked harder now while we were younger, we would reap the rewards (I guess that's the lucky part to the above quote) sooner in our lives. In our case, his work got him killed! I had to come to terms with the fact that Lyndon would NEVER see any of our hard work getting paid off or make us "lucky."

I feel I may put a few noses out of joint by saying this, but losing a loved one in this way is inexplicable. They weren't sick. It was untimely and out of order in so many ways, not to mention the array of professional bodies who now have to get involved. It's hard. It's difficult. It's cruel. It's simply needless!

It is a common misconception that when somebody is killed in a workplace incident, the bereaved family automatically becomes some sort of instant overnight "millionaire." But that mistaken belief couldn't be further from the truth, and to be honest, absolutely pisses me off to no end! Can you feel the frustration in my words yet?

I have had so many people assume that, due to the company's prosecution of over $1 million, that it is given to the families who were involved. That, again, couldn't be further from the truth. Again, in this case, the prosecution does not involve the victims' families like you would expect. It is all fact-driven and between SafeWork and the company. I have had friends who asked, "Are you good now, I mean financially?"

Like seriously, what the actual F#%!! I know it was probably coming from a good place. But, ummm, no. The number of misguided comments was astronomical, absurd, and downright degrading to the life of my husband. There was no need, however, to inform them of the reality because they simply would not have been able to comprehend the complexity that goes with losing your loved one through a workplace incident.

Now this goes against all my beliefs, as Lyndon and I would NEVER talk about our personal financial situation. The fact, however, is that because this incident was so public, many people felt the need to ask. And it's just downright bloody rude! The reason I am telling this is more so to shed light on this and, hopefully, to inform people reading this that if you ever must deal with this, please DON'T ASK any financial questions to the family involved. Not only is it rude, as I said before, but you will almost always find yourself being excluded from this family even if you are a friend or close contact. It is no one's business other than the people directly involved. Money doesn't make it better nor dissolve the pain.

Yes, we were compensated, so to speak. However, the level of compensation will NEVER be enough when you are talking about the needless death of your husband, father, son, or brother. What people fail to understand, in our case, Lyndon was only 35.... He had over 30 years of work still left in him, and those funds need to last 30+ years. The figure of compensation for the death of a worker within NSW does not change based on your status (i.e. single or with children). It does not change based on the age of the deceased (i.e., a 35-year-old or a 62-year-old.) I believe the amount remains the same. This amount, regulated by the State Insurance Regulatory authority (SIRA), is a once-off lump sum.

This lump sum only goes to those dependents of the deceased. My children and I only. What was going through my mind was, what about parents or siblings? How is that fair? How is that justice? How is that possible??

Depending on which jurisdiction in Australia your loved one died (in our case, NSW) will also change how much you get. I am a firm believer, everyone, regardless of whether they were in NSW, or QLD, or WA, should be entitled to the same amount. A good friend of mine, who lives in a different state, would often speak with me about the irregularities of such a failing system.

The Australian Institute of Family Studies (AIFS) released a publication back in 2018 on the estimated costs of raising children. Now that we are 7 years post that date, this figure would have changed drastically due to inflation, I am sure, but it gives you a glimpse. To find out more, you can go to the aifs.gov.au website. This media release shows that the average costs of raising a child are between $140-$170 a week. That, mind you, is researched on the unemployed and low-income families (not mid-range or high income). So theoretically, if we base this on the upside of the scale at $170, that is just under $9k a year for one child. Say you are raising 2 children, for example, that is $17,680 per year. Now, let's assume you were raising them for 12 years after the death of a husband, that's a whopping $212k. Again, that figure is based on the bare minimum and was published 7 years prior, so that figure is only going to grow.

Now (with the above figures and knowledge in our mind), let's assume you had both of your 2 kids plus yourself in regular psychology or counselling sessions, depression medication ongoing, reviews, etc. Not only is this already difficult to deal with, it becomes a financial nightmare! All 100% preventable. The death of a loved one and impact on the mental health of everyone else involved is eye watering.

When you are thrust into this new world, not only are you trying to grieve the loss, but you are also dealing with so much more. As a wife, I was grieving, not just my husband, but our entire future life that we had planned together. PTSD, depression, and trauma also crept in very quickly, which led to cognitive decline. This then meant giving up my job and, in turn, losing my income and along with what was left of my sanity. Well over half a decade on, I still regularly see a psychologist which, if you have ever seen a specialist, you know are not cheap. I will probably require therapy for my remaining years and no compensation is given for that.

For what you have to endure lifelong, it's actually an insult and I can assure you, I myself had a word (actually blurted out whilst in the midst of a total meltdown) to my solicitor at this time saying it's insulting that a monetary value can be put on someone's life. And just about every person I have spoken to in the same boat have said they were of the same opinion. It's another kick to the guts whilst in our moments of deep grief.

Get it now?? Nope, you never would until you have lived this, and as I said before, we don't want that happening because that would mean another needless workplace death.

When Lyndon passed away, I had to learn to do so many things. I did honestly feel like a child again. When it came to driving anywhere, Lyndon was always the driver and absolutely loved it. It is probably a male thing, because other than driving around town I did not really drive. Now I had to learn to stand on my own two feet, and as silly as it sounds, driving was such a trigger for me that I would go into full-blown panic attacks, even if just driving for 1 hour down the highway. I had to push past my fear, obviously, and now, I can say that I drive everywhere without a problem. Well, almost anywhere. It really is small tasks, like distance driving, that I feel proud of because I have been able to overcome this.

A MOMENT OF REFLECTION

To everyone who reads this – please sort your legal shit out.

In Australia, you need to be 18 years old (with minor exceptions to that rule) to get a will. As a young family, we did not have a will. I was always sceptical of getting a will so young as it almost felt like it would "curse" us. Silly, I know, especially because in my line of work we asked clients if they had a will. In hindsight, I wish I had organised this sooner. As part of my work in the superannuation and accounting industry, I looked at this information as a necessity for obvious reasons. Having a will in place would have made the aftermath of Lyndon's death less of an administrative burden.

One of the most important things I believe you can do is get a legal will drawn up as soon as you are eligible. As my son turns 18 and Mia in a couple of years, this will form part of their birthday present. Even as youngsters, they are not exempt from the curveballs life will throw at them, and they have witnessed that already. With their wills in place, I will be able to rest assured that their individual wishes are taken into account just as they would have wanted. Even if you don't have much to your name, a legal will, in my eyes, is a must. Please consider this for yourself, your kids, whomever is legally eligible. Go and get advice appropriate to you and your circumstances for your peace of mind.

Another thing in Australia is Superannuation. Again, we were lucky that, working in the finance and superannuation industry, ours was updated regularly. Please ensure you seek proper legal and financial advice for your superannuation and how that would look in the event of your untimely death. Not to mention, if your personal circumstances change, seek advice accordingly. Your benefits may be paid to the wrong person or get into the wrong hands. I have heard of way too many stories of this happening. So, please, ensure you seek advice to ensure it's in line with YOUR wishes.

REFLECTION QUESTIONS:

1. Do you have a current and valid will? If not, why not?

2. When was the last time you reviewed your superannuation's beneficiary?
   Many people don't know about this or overlook this which I believe is a big mistake. Seek appropriate advice and get it sorted.

3. Do you have a good solicitor who you would trust to turn to if an event happens?
   Not all solicitors are the same in area of expertise.

CHAPTER 10

FAILURES TURNED INTO LEARNINGS

"Education is the most powerful weapon which you can use to change the world."

– NELSON MANDELA

A further and very confronting matter was sitting through the court case and the handing down of the sentence. I wanted to be there in person so badly, but due to the hard border closures throughout COVID times, this was unworkable. So it was over the internet, but better than nothing, right? Obviously, the whole damn thing was confronting. And we all know, we shouldn't have had to go through what we did. I am of the very strong opinion that this system is a broken one and there is no justice for the victims and their families whatsoever. You can ask the many people who have gone before me and I know they will give you a similar story.

That being said, Oprah Winfrey so famously said, *"Turn your wounds into wisdom."*

The failings of this particular incident can be developed into wisdom, so that there will be no other workplace incident of its kind in the future. I know for damn sure that Lyndon would not want anyone else to go through what he went through or what his family (us) goes through each and every day. I can't live knowing his life was in vain!

I don't want to go into blame here. Rather, I am trying to find a positive outlet from such a tragedy and the failings below prove a prime example of learning from such a tragic and needless incident. As it came out in the handing down of the sentence in September 2020 (just shy of 2.5 years after the incident), the following failures were evidenced. The workplace had failed to:

1. Define the top of the tank as a confined space or restricted area, although workers had ready access by way of a ladder to the area.

2. Eliminate or minimise the formation of Hydrogen Sulphide (H2S) in storage tanks with filtrate.

3. Supply workers with personal hazardous gas monitors.

4. Provide all workers with the appropriate training for possible exposure to hazardous gases (such as H2S) at the worksite.

5. Ensure adequate ventilation to the basement area of the paper machine.
6. Deliver a system to observe and record the stored filtrate, thus safeguarding the risk to health of employees from built up levels of Hydrogen Sulphide gas.

The first learning, which should be a no-brainer to someone with a WHS background, is about the tank which the men climbed on top of. The tank was about 5m in height and above the tank, where the men were, was not designed for human occupation. It was a so-called "crawl space." So, armed with that knowledge, the question that came to my mind was why a ladder was fixed to the side if you were not supposed to access the top of it? The employer company did end up removing the ladder following the incident.

One of my first questions was, "Was this a designated confined space?" Which received a resounding "No." We later came to understand that the inside of the tank itself was an assigned confined space, but the top of the tank had no access restrictions, nor was it treated as a confined space. The judge also mentioned that it was actually challenging to remove an unconscious person. In our case, if this area were deemed a confined space, then the required cards, permits, and assessments would have been carried out, right? In my opinion, our men would then definitely still be here today.

Another take away is about the H2S gas, which is a byproduct of many industries, including pulp and paper manufacturing. This is the first learning opportunity. It was not fully known (going by the people I asked at the time) that this gas had the potential to be so catastrophic, let alone deadly. We all knew of the "rotten egg" smell, but did not think anything sinister of it. But clearly, it has the potential to KILL. So the application from this learning is to train your employees about all RISKS pertaining to any hazardous substances that may or even have the slightest risk of harm to human life. It may just save a life or 3!!!

Numbers 3 and 4 from the list are another gigantic failing in my eyes, and it is my honest and personal opinion that given the correct gas monitors and training when working in this specific area, our men would be here today. PPE Gas monitors should have been fixed to all employees when entering mid to high risk areas, as well as a fixed gas monitor on or above the tank, which ties into number 6 as well. I am of the understanding that prior to the incident taking place, it was noted that gas monitors were in fact used to detect several gases, including H2S. However, the monitors were only in the designated confined spaces. This meant that the inside of the tank had a monitor, but not at the top. I believe this would have given added risk mitigation in case one of the monitors was faulty. Other similar worksites have these available.

In this specific case, the company was also ordered to make an animated video of the incident for training purposes, and in May 2025, I was able to muster up the courage to watch this video for the first time. It is an absolute joke in my opinion. An animation?! To me, it sounds impersonal. A cartoon was made from this tragedy. It is yet another kick to the guts for me. Although I am not keen on the idea (as I just stated - I'm looking at this video from the grieving widow's side), I can see the benefits for certain industries. So from a training perspective, I am all for it.

A MOMENT OF REFLECTION

As I have mentioned previously, if you try to look at things positively, and I for one know how difficult this can be, we can take learning outcomes from every situation we face. If we remove all the noise and go back to the bare basics, we can ask ourselves so many questions to better any future outcomes.

Safety learnings are an obvious one, but also a very easy one, and if the safety measures were in place, I believe our men would still be here. All companies can actually take away these safety learnings, thus making it safer for their own employees.

REFLECTION QUESTIONS:

1. Have a think about what happened today for you personally. What are some learnings (whether the situation was good or bad) that you can take away?

2. Place yourself in a work situation. Reflect and think, do you have a degree or a licence to do what you do? Do you think you need those qualifications to give you wisdom or to make an impact?

3. Use your voice to speak up at work. If you are reprimanded for doing so, the culture is shit, and you should seek alternative employment, in my opinion. Your safety is paramount!

4. If you work in any site with confined spaces (or not), I urge you to rethink all spaces. Think outside the box. Are there any new machines, fittings, etc. that may have not been adequately assigned as a confined space?

CHAPTER 11

A DAY FOR ALL WORKERS

"Heroes never die. They live on in the hearts and minds of those who would follow in their footsteps."

– EMILY POTTER

A friend once said to me, who lost her son, "I've learnt that grief rearranges your address book." That saying is ever so true and has stuck with me ever since. Grief is such a cruel feeling/emotion, yet grief is the price we pay for love.

My family learned very quickly that there is actually an international Memorial Day for workers just like Lyndon. This is known as Worker's Memorial Day, or it can sometimes also be known as International Commemoration Day (ICD) for Dead and Injured or National Day of Mourning. It is set on the 28th of April each year. The purple ribbon is also used to signify remembrance of this important date.

On the 28th of April each year workers and their loved ones from all over the globe come together to pay their respects to the workers, just trying to make an honest living, who have been killed on the job or who are seriously injured or made unwell by their line of work. Memorial Day is recognised nationally in various countries, including but not limited to: Australia, Brazil, the US, UK, Canada & Spain. There are still a few countries, I believe, that are yet to follow suit and gain traction, and hopefully very soon they will be on board, but you can see how widespread across the world this movement is already.

It's a poignant reminder that, as a society, especially in a first world country like ours, enough is not being done to save our people, our greatest asset – our workers! It's the modern age, people! I strongly believe that there shouldn't be any workers still being killed at work, and therefore this day shouldn't need to exist. I can't stress enough that it's an absolute necessity to strengthen the significance of increasing awareness when it comes to the avoidance of health and safety within the workplace across all jurisdictions and across all industries.

So the 28th of April is yet another difficult day for me and our family. It's a loud reminder that he is gone forever, never to return. Having the other families, who have unfortunately been dealt the same cards, also attend so we can cry together, laugh together, and share stories of our loved ones, is ultimately what gets me through this day each and every year.

In 2019, there was an unveiling of the plaque in Albury/Wodonga, Victoria, Australia (our home town), and it had the names of Lyndon and his colleagues who died alongside him. An emotional day to say the least. Every year, I have attended this event without fail, whether it be in Wodonga, online (during COVID), or in Brisbane, Australia.

I witnessed the most beautiful church ceremony in Brisbane's CBD a few years back, and the comradery of all workers in their high-vis uniforms was just a statement in itself. Attending a large cathedral in Brisbane's CBD in 2023 was a moment I will never forget. The church was beautiful and so very big. We had the first few rows designated for affected families so it was slightly intimidating walking past hundreds of workers. And I mean hundreds. The church was jam-packed and they even had a screen outside across the road in the park where hundreds more workers filled the park. The speeches they had were powerful, and the songs that they played - well, let's just say one was also played at Lyndon's funeral so I was a complete mess.

But what made it ever so special was that they had a wreath-laying at the end, where every person in attendance was given the opportunity to place a single rose, beginning with the affected families (us) first. Watching each and every worker in their high-vis attire walk up and give their own unique moment of silence. One gentleman walked up and sat on the floor in front while taking a moment, bowing his head to the wreath, getting up, and then turning to us and bowing. It sends shivers down my spine, in a beautiful way, just thinking about it. It really was the most moving day in a heartbreaking way (apart from Lyndon's funeral) I had ever witnessed.

A MOMENT OF REFLECTION

The main reflection here is to think about all our workers who are needlessly being killed on the work watch. I urge you, whether you know someone personally or not who has been affected, to mark

> the 28th of April in your calendar, just as you would for any other significantly marked day. If you can attend one of these days, or even do anything to show your awareness of this day, it says so much to families like mine who live this. Post a post to your socials on this day, wear a purple ribbon, anything to show your support for our number one asset – our workers!

REFLECTION QUESTIONS:

1. Let me ask you, do you know of anyone who has died while at their place of work?
   If so, were they close to you or an acquaintance?

2. Could you mark just 1 hour out of your day on the 28th April to attend Workers Memorial Day?
   If you attend one of these days, it's very difficult not to get emotional and realise how big this day really is and what it truly signifies. I'd love for you to send me a message and tell me about your experience.

An image of the memorial in Wodonga, Victoria, where our men and others who died at work are remembered

My photo for the Worker's Memorial Day

CHAPTER 12

A BELLY FULL OF FIRE

"And one day she discovered that she was fierce, and strong, and full of fire, and that not even she could hold herself back because her passion burned brighter than her fears."

– MARK ANTHONY

For that first year, it is safe to say that I was very reserved. (I know, not like me at all, right?!) But in my defence, we had so much outside noise going on around us whilst we were still just trying to comprehend what the hell had just happened. The media were relentless, going to any length to get a statement, but I kept relatively quiet for the sake of our family.

Feeling entirely beaten and overwhelmed, I found the most comfort in isolation. I had opted to embrace, to a certain extent, a reclusive way of life, which was now my coping mechanism. My days would be made up of the norm of placing the kids on the school bus, followed by disappearing back to bed until they came home in the afternoon. This cycle became a daily routine, offering somewhat a sense of comfort during times that seemed to be taxing, difficult, and never-ending.

To be completely honest, I tried drinking but didn't get too far, as I have never been a big drinker. I did think about drugs and other substances to numb the pain, and the thought of taking my life crossed my mind. However, I chose not to go down that road because I had my beautiful children and I made a promise to Lyndon. Remember, when Lyndon was on his deathbed (quite literally), I promised him that I would never give up. I have the rest of my life to live and make him proud!

But by the first anniversary of his death, I was deep in my heartache and anguish. Despite this, I could feel the anger beginning to bubble over. The investigation was taking so bloody long from where I was standing. I felt it was not as much of a priority for them as it was for our family. I really did not want to get in the way of the investigation as I wanted the company brought to account by any means possible. But witnessing firsthand the brokenness of a system that is supposed to protect our workers, I could see not much was being done other than failure to the families such as my own.

In speaking to other people who had been in my shoes already, they all had similar thought patterns to me. So it was then I decided enough was enough. I could not sit down whilst everyone else went about their normal day. So, my fight for change, justice, and accountability had begun. This is the time I first acknowledged there was a fire in my belly.

So many thoughts were running through my head, "Are we just supposed to roll over and accept this? Is this all that life is worth when push comes to shove? In a society like we live in today, how can killing workers still be happening at all?"

We need answers! We are supposed to be living in a first-world country, but what I realise now is that there is no "first world" when it comes to workplace safety. I could not and still can not get over the fact that approximately 200 worker deaths a year are happening in Australia. WTF? Right under our noses. This number is staggering. My thought was, what are the regulators doing?

I had done a couple of media interviews by this stage, and I had gotten an appointment with a few people higher up. I remember sitting in one Parliamentary member's boardroom with my mum accompanying me. She listened but, as she was not in a position to assist, put me onto another member of parliament. Through talks with him, he managed to secure an appointment with the Minister at the time. And so this is where my journey of speaking up began.

At this point in time, I was regularly speaking to the mother of the young man who had passed alongside Lyndon. I had told her that I was going to Sydney, and she asked if she could come with me. I believed that the more people in this fight, the better, and we became a united front. So, off we toddled to Sydney, with photos of our men in tow. We sat in the Minister's office in Parliament House and laid it on the table; we did not hold back. The friendship that comes from a tragedy like this is unexplainable. I formed a close bond with the other ladies from this tragedy also.

It was around mid 2020, and I couldn't handle the feelings and emotions that were shadowing me, seeing the billows of steam spewing out of the stacks from the mill were a constant reminder. So, despite saying I would never sell our forever family home, I found myself doing just that. I sold our beautiful home full of memories that we had created and found myself moving 13 hours across states to the sunshine state of QLD. That was in the midst of COVID, so you can probably gather the obstacles that we endured, such as the QLD border hard shutdowns.

Even though I had officially sold our house in NSW, we had 3 days to pack up our lives rather than the weeks we originally had planned. I was told that if we were not over the NSW/QLD border by 12am, we would be turned around and locked out. This difficulty is a time forever etched into my memory, but it is nothing compared to what we had been dealing with, so I was not fazed and just went with the flow. I honestly never thought I would be living anywhere other than our home in Albury, and I suppose that taught me that you should never say never! I often ask myself if I made the right decision. And I guess I will never know the answer. But I was doing what I needed to do at the time, and I do love where we are living now.

One of the hardest things I have had to do since making that decision is telling my in-laws. They are our everything, but I had to do what I felt was right for my children and me. I was crying when I told them, because I was so petrified as I thought they would not see me as their daughter-in-law now that their son was gone. I honestly don't know why – I guess it's just the thought and so much fear of losing them too. I don't know what I would do without them. They were naturally upset, but they knew deep down that I had to go. I couldn't live in Albury at that time; I had to be closer to my mother. However, one thing was certain, they are and always will be my strength, and I love them with all my heart.

Towards the end of 2020, I was a founding member of a NSW support group that advises the government from our experience. Having already moved to Queensland, I travelled down to NSW for the meetings. This group had its ups and downs. However, I knew that as a collective, we were determined to make the most of the voices we each had to get our individual messages of safety out into the public realm. After numerous different officials had moved through the group's leadership, I felt this was not doing the group any favours nor did I feel we were moving forward in the direction that the group was intended.

It was then that both I and another member were appointed as Co-Chairs of this group, and we quickly started to gain momentum and traction.

In the years that followed, more leadership personnel changes happened, and a couple of us felt that we were no-longer gaining any traction, so it was then that my fellow Co-chair and I decided to tender our resignations simultaneously (to make a stand) and left the group in late 2024. For me, this time on my journey was an eye opener on so many levels, but I personally felt controlled by the red tape, and I needed to make some serious changes, on a personal level. The reason I became involved in this group was to make positive changes so nobody else endured such tragedy, but once I felt these changes were not happening, it was time for the fire in my belly to explode!

Obviously, I feel extremely passionate about this, and there is absolutely no way in hell that I will allow Lyndon's name to be used as a box-ticking exercise. It was my time to step aside into something much bigger and way out of my comfort zone. So, it was then, I went out on my own. At the start of 2025, I began pushing hard to grow my following on my social media networks, whilst also focusing on my budding business and directly educating businesses and their workers without barriers or red tape.

In 2023, the stats of workplace fatalities in Australia alone were a whopping 200 people killed. This information was drawn from the Safe Work Australia publication and website. If you break that down, every 1.8 days somebody is killed at work (for the purposes of this book, I will round to the nearest decimal of 2). This means that there is a needless workplace death every 2 days in a so-called first-world country with apparently second-to-none safety legislation! It is absolutely appalling!

In 2022, there were approx. 195 fatalities.

In 2021, there were approx. 172 fatalities.

In 2020, there were approx. 194 fatalities.

In 2019, there were approx. 183 fatalities.

In 2018, there were approx. 144 fatalities – Lyndon and his colleague are included in this count!

Now, I am sorry, but on what planet is that okay or justifiable? If your loved one formed part of this count, would you just sit back and say "We have good rules and regulations?"

I do not think so. I say that my husband and every other worker are everyday people like you and me. They are NOT statistics. But for the purposes of writing this book and trying to point out the industrial fatality rate, this was the clearest list I could muster. The above awful data doesn't even include those who are seriously injured, narrowly avoiding a death sentence, nor those that take their own lives after the fact of the incident. And let me tell you, this additional number is just as staggering.

Quite frankly, I don't think it is okay for our workers or their families to put up with this. Under Australian WHS laws, all workers have a right to a safe and healthy working environment and I believe that includes safely coming home to their loved ones at the end of a shift – no exceptions! This is a basic human right!

A MOMENT OF REFLECTION

I may harp on a bit sometimes, but again, I learned the power of "Never say never." I can only hope that someone is reading my book (whether living a similar situation or not) and takes power from this, knowing that there is something bigger out there for them. You, too, have the ability to make a difference in this world and make it a better place for the next generation.

It is certainly easy to run with the whole "poor me" perception after such a tragedy. And let me tell you, I was great at this. I felt my life was just a game of bad cards being dealt, one after another. There are certainly times that I still think about what I could have done to deserve all that was thrown at us. But in reality, so many people are going through their own stories of tragedy, and we just don't know about it. As they say, just be kind to everyone because you don't know what anyone is dealing with on a personal level.

One thing I have learnt along the way is that "lived experience" CAN be used for a much greater cause. It is a lived experience because you lived through it and you survived it, despite it trying to break you. You have gained knowledge and wisdom from it. You now have the power to use this to help other people, should you choose that path. Don't think it will never happen to you, because that thought process in itself is complacency and complacency kills!

I would like to think that through adversity, resilience was born, and it's my job to share that with the world. Lyndon's legacy made me see life through a different lens. He was the kindest person you would ever meet. So the fact that such a wonderful man had such an undeserved death, my friends, is what gives me the fire in my belly to keep sharing and, hopefully, save lives.

REFLECTION QUESTIONS:

1. The term 'never say never' has certainly resonated with me over the years and by reading my story, I'm sure most of you could resonate with the saying.
   What resonates with you the most when you hear this phrase?

2. I believe we all have a fire in our belly waiting to be sparked. For me, it was obviously losing my best friend and husband. Has yours been ignited or sparked? If so, why? If not, what do you think it would take to ignite such a fire?

3. We all have a voice. How would you use your voice to become powerful and inspire others, if given the chance?

4. What can you do to make sure you don't become complacent in your work or everyday life?

TRAGEDY: Husband and father-of-two Lyndon Quinlivan died in the accident. Tributes flowed after his death, with one noting 'his last act was that of a workplace hero'.

Border Mail Snippet of Lyndon

TUESDAY DECEMBER 03, 2019

bordermail.com.au

$1.70

The Border Mail

Every second of every day

The widow of a worker killed at Norske Skog hopes that legal action by SafeWork NSW will save other families from the agony of losing a loved one. Norske Skog has been charged with workplace health and safety breaches after the deaths of Lyndon Quinlivan and Ben Pascall at the paper mill in May last year. Mr Quinlivan's wife Jacci has spoken publicly for the first time, sharing the ongoing grief at the loss of her husband and father of their two children. "It absolutely doesn't get any easier," she said. "It hurts every second of every day, everything is a reminder of what has been taken from myself, our children, his parents, his sister, my parents, the list goes on."

BLAIR THOMSON report, another MARK JESSER picture: P6

Border Mail photo, 2019. Every second of every day

NEWS

Tragedy 'could have been avoided' at mill

Border Mail photo, 2020. Tragedy could have been avoided

CHAPTER 13

OUT ON MY OWN

"Be responsible for telling people the truth. Not managing people's reactions to it."

– MEL ROBBINS

In paying tribute to the cherished legacy that is my husband's, this book serves as a testament to enduring memories, challenges and lessons learned. This book's pages embrace my raw and significant story with a narrative powered by a profound pledge to share experiences that resonate with many.

My aim is clear: protecting workers' well-being by shedding light on the many challenges faced on worksites and offering a ray of light or beacon of hope for a brighter future for all the people of Australia and around the world. Through my personal words, my hope is to pave a path forward that spares others the suffering we have known all too well and continue to navigate.

> *"A champion is one who is remembered.*
> *A legend is one who is never forgotten."*
> – Matshona Dhliwayo

After making the huge decision (not a hard one) in late 2024 to begin my journey as a public speaker and safety advocate, things started to evolve naturally. Storytelling using my own lived experience allows me to express myself, using my vulnerability to shed light on this vital topic. Storytelling can connect to people, whereas statistics cannot always do that. Many have inquired why I choose to share my story of tragedy. My answer is simple – because it is Lyndon's legacy. I will say it until I am blue in the face – I am Lyndon's voice! I cannot stand by and watch more people being killed and their families' lives turned upside down when there's something that I could do to save even just one life.

I share my personal story whilst sharing safety messages because the story, as difficult as it is to relive, shares a profound message of hope around safety. There is approximately one person every two days being needlessly killed in workplace incidents across Australia alone. Imagine if that were your husband, your father, your parent, your sibling, or even your best mate? I'm sure that many who are reading this, if the shoe were on the other foot, would want to make that loved one's legacy live on through guiding people so it doesn't happen to anyone else. Am I right?

I share our story to give a voice to those who may not be able to speak up for various reasons, whatever they may be. Workplace safety is crucial and absolutely vital. It's disheartening that so many are part of this club when no one wishes to join. Let's remember that workplace fatalities and injuries are PREVENTABLE. My aim and mission are to work together with those willing to ensure a safe work environment for all workers.

I couldn't have believed that this is where I would be 7 years along in my journey. Public speaking almost became an excitement. I never in my wildest dreams envisioned that I would say that. It scares the absolute beejesus out of me while, at the same time, there is something in knowing I am getting this vital message spread wider to the public and businesses that value their number #1 asset – Workers. Playing a major role in that leads to fulfilling my life's purpose, as explained at the beginning of this story.

It's been amazing to see my following grow steadily, predominantly on LinkedIn. Another moment of gratitude to all my followers. The engagement from followers has been unexpected, but incredibly rewarding. I am wholeheartedly grateful for the connections made and the conversations sparked.

In June, 2025, I did my very first podcast in the safety realm for an international company. I was quietly shitting my pants if I am being honest. I really don't know why I was so nervous because it wasn't as though I had never publicly spoken about this topic, but I most certainly was. The host had the utmost professional and calming demeanour, and once I began speaking with him, he made me feel instantly at ease. As he is in the safety space and has a worldwide following, he knew what I was talking about instantly. He even did his research prior to our first meeting. Once the recording was over, it was like a wave of confidence that came over me. The fact that my story is now going global and I am raising awareness on this important issue surrounding safety is a silver lining.

When I heard it back, obviously, I had some very harsh self-criticism. But I decided to take it on the chin as it was my very first podcast, and I am sure there will be others to come. So, as I do, I will take it as constructive learning and build from it. I have also received some very positive feedback, so I know I am hitting the mark, and the message is going where it needs to go. Again, I am attracting a global audience in Lyndon's honour – a pivotal moment in my personal life. I eagerly anticipate many more podcasts in the coming years.

In the same month, I had my first large-client presentation. Again, I've spoken before to hundreds of people, but I guess I had people I knew there for moral support. That's the only thing I could think about as to why my nerves were so high. One thing I know, and I have always said, is my calling - to use the pain in a positive way to help people. So it's not a matter of "I can't do this" but instead a matter of "I must do this."

I went into this meeting with my head held high, and for the first 5 minutes, I could feel and hear the nervousness in my voice. It was shaky and almost like I had just run a marathon and couldn't catch my breath. I know my nerves were visible, but I owned it. Why? Because I deserved to be here spreading the message of safety. As I always do, I put the nerves down to learning. I'm not a born public speaker, so that's just another thing I add to my to-do list – practise until it's god-damn perfect.

> *"If you really want to do something, you'll find a way.*
> *If you don't, you'll find an excuse."*
> – Jim Rohn

This quote deeply resonates with me on so many levels. This was the type of go-getter that Lyndon was (he'd always find a way) but moreso, it sticks with me from the standpoint of my mission which is to seek change. Nothing will stand in my way.

It was a small crowd, maybe 15 people, with a few more attending online. I remember there was one person who looked like he didn't want to be there and even looked like we were keeping him awake. But I remembered what a good friend once told me: there will always be that one person in the audience. What gave me hope that my message was getting through was the four people sitting to the right of me. Their gaze was fixed on me for nearly the whole of the presentation. When I'd say certain things, the looks on their faces changed. And the interaction when I'd pose a question - they were intrigued and answering with a shake or nod of the head. That was what I wanted. Engagement. And that's what I got. When I wrapped up my presentation, half left to get morning tea and half stayed back to talk. The question I received, again, is why I do what I do. My answer was because I know my message got through and safety is at the forefront of their minds, yet again.

My son is currently in his final year of secondary schooling at an industry trade college. I have built a rapport with the school whereby they have invited me in to share my story, multiple times to multiple cohorts of students. First and foremost, Chris is okay with this as he understands the importance of why I share this story. New students at this school go through a rigorous program before they can go out to work experience or obtain school-based apprenticeships. It really is the best program I have gotten my son into and Lyndon would be proud of his achievements, just as I am. This relationship poses a great opportunity to get my message out to the younger and more vulnerable cohorts of students.

The challenge that I could see here, was that I would be presenting to a large group of teenage students who are approximately 15 – 18 years of age. Can you remember when you were this age? I know I can. I thought I was invincible. Because they are almost ready to be leaving school and entering the workforce, they are naturally considered a higher-risk worker when it comes to workplace health and safety. In fact, for Queensland statistics alone, approximately 4,400 young people who are aged between 15 and 24 are seriously injured each year. Now, how do I get across my story to them, whilst trying not to scare the absolute pants off them? This is a challenge I accepted head-on and I was pleasantly surprised. These young people are eager to learn and hungry for information about the workforce.

This has meant that I have needed to change my whole presentation, as kids are at a different learning level, which is obvious. But it's also still a school environment and my normal presentation did touch on the mental health of workers and suicide. My thought process was that a lot of parents would certainly not want someone talking about that topic to their children. I know I certainly was one of those parents, at least up until our incident. Then I changed that view completely and I am quite open with the kids about a lot of stuff. My kids had dealt with the unimaginable at a very young age. What worse could they need to deal with?

Again, I looked at this as an ideal opportunity to not only get out there and bring to the forefront of workers' and apprentices' minds, but also to instill the message of safety into our young and vulnerable workers. I now have a few presentations for different audience levels which has been extremely beneficial for my business. It is my hope that other schools will jump on this so I can drum in this safety message even further. Another door has certainly been unlocked over the past 6 months!

I have had the amazing opportunity to go on a "breakfast roadshow" with my dear friend Patrizia (whom I will speak about more in the next chapter) and share our stories of tragedy with many. The roadshow consisted of us travelling for a week to certain regional centres in NSW, where we would hold the presentation early in the morning whilst the attendees had breakfast before going on to continue their normal workday. We presented our stories and the real ramifications of what life looks like for us now. The goal is that their mindsets change and they are left with the safety topic at the forefront of their minds.

A MOMENT OF REFLECTION

Far too often, people don't speak up for whatever reason that may be. One of the most powerful tools each and every one of us has is the power of our voice. For whatever reason, be it about safety, about morals, about family, or a cause close to your heart, you HAVE a voice. And you are well within your rights to use it! Bigger things may be unlocked for you that you never dreamed possible, and ultimately, you will touch the hearts of someone out there.

> *"I challenge you to step outside your comfort zone and use your voice."*
> – J. Quinlivan

REFLECTION QUESTIONS:

1. Is something happening at work that doesn't sit right with you? STOP what you are doing immediately and speak up. Report it.

2. Have you just gone through a health battle (my stroke, for example) and you want to let others know or make them aware, use your voice. I challenge you to step outside your comfort zone and use your voice. You will feel empowered, confident, and thankful that you have been able to potentially help someone. I'm offering to be your accountability partner. Get in contact with me and tell me how you used your voice and, in turn, how it made you feel.

3. What are you waiting for? If you want to do something, be it public speaking or a new career, practise, practise, practise. Practise until you are satisfied, then practise some more.

Presenting at the 2026 Workplace Health and Safety Show in Brisbane

Jacqueline Quinlivan Logo and tag

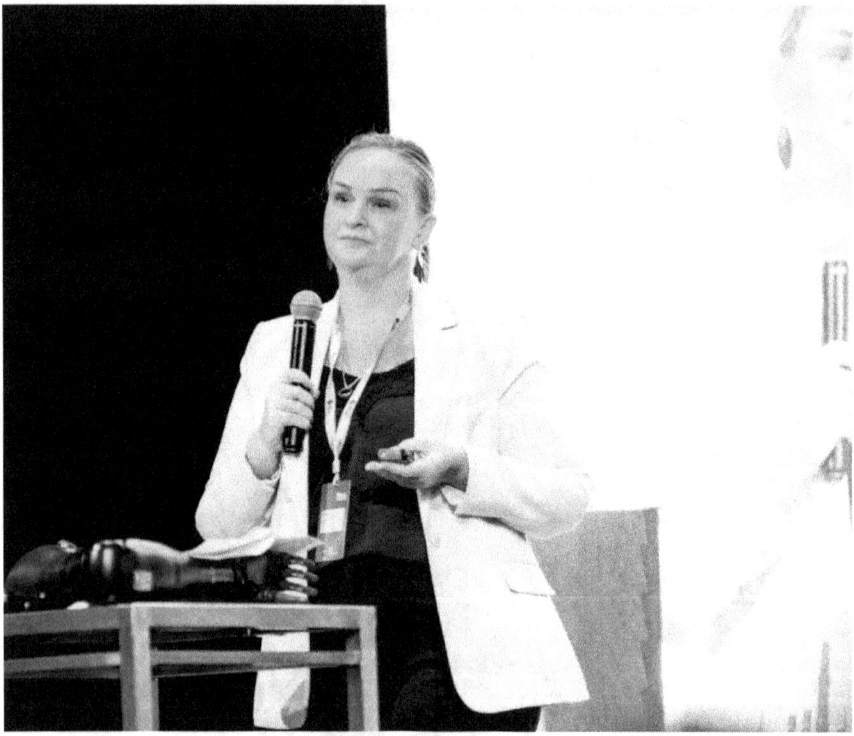

Speaking at the 2026 National Safety Conference in Sydney.
Photo by NSCA Foundation

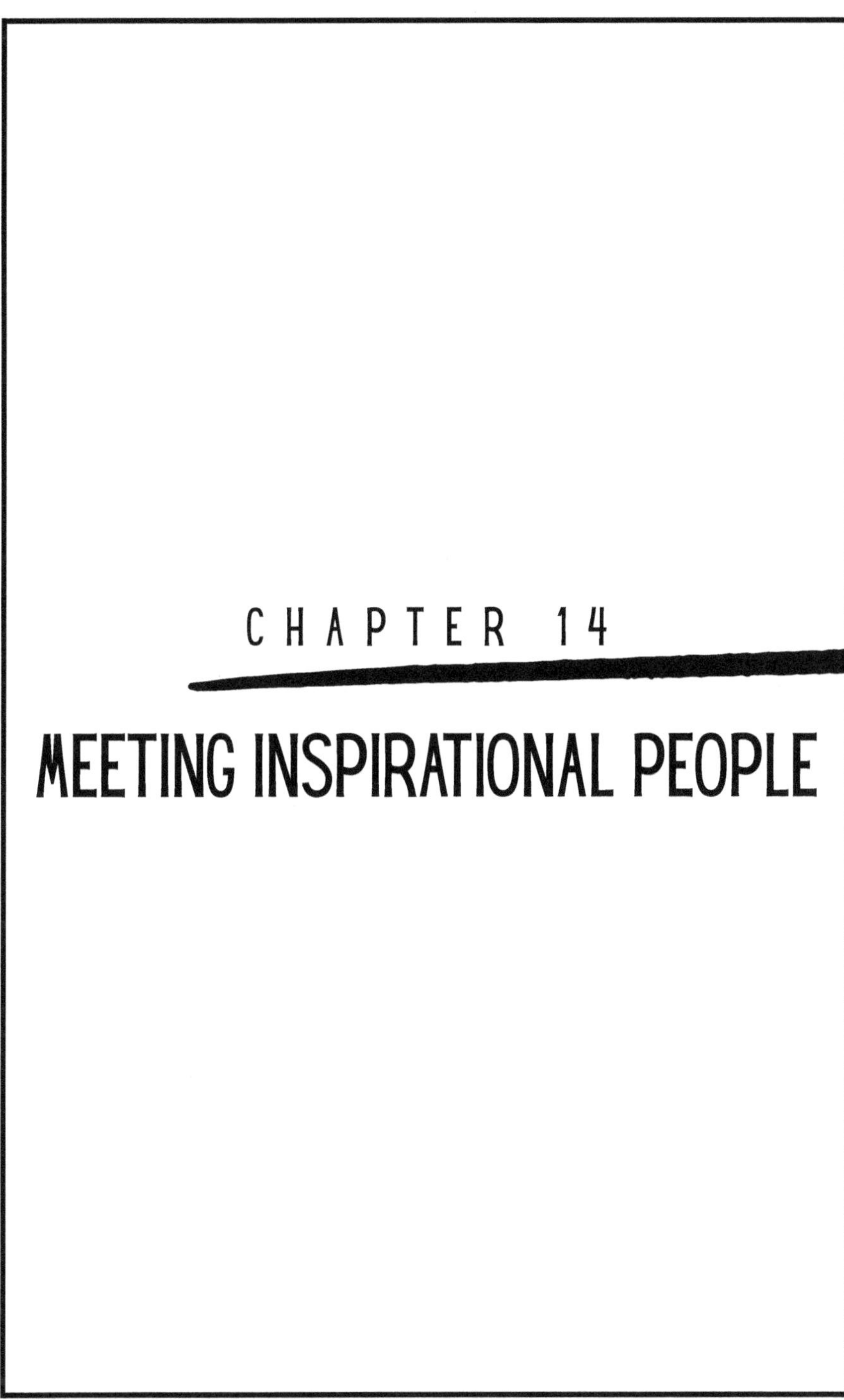

CHAPTER 14

MEETING INSPIRATIONAL PEOPLE

"Your circle should want to see you win. Your circle should clap the loudest when you have good news. If they don't, get a new circle."

– WESLEY SNIPES

After the incident, it is safe to say that my world went dark. Throughout this period, I have learnt and am still learning to be grateful for the small things as well as the large things in life. Gratitude is strongly associated with a deeper level and understanding of true happiness, and this has been researched in positive psychology. I will not lie, there are days when I am not feeling grateful and I am feeling triggered, sad, down, and that's okay. I have learnt to let my grief travel with me, as no matter what, it will be there anyway. But it's the gratitude that ALWAYS gets me feeling better about myself and moving forward with life because, ultimately, that's what Lyndon would want for me.

Being a mother, you would do anything for your kids, that's an obvious one. However, never would I have imagined my own mum doing everything that she has done for me. She loved Lyndon like there was no tomorrow, so she was grieving the loss of her son-in-law. Now, having to comfort her young, widowed daughter and her grandkids, she was in full force. Mum had become the person I confided in when that was once Lyndon. Putting her down on medical forms as my next of kin again was beyond HARD as that was supposed to be Lyndon. The executor for my will, Mum again. And although I am ever so grateful, it's just another reminder of everything we have had to endure. Her presence gave me the ability to focus on grieving while she was accompanying me to all my appointments and managing household chores to ensure my children were cared for when I couldn't get up off the lounge because of my level of shock. Her unwavering assistance was a literal lifeline. In those initial weeks (and to this very day), her nurturing presence created a sense of comfort and stability when my world was obliterated. Mum is my rock and she is one of the most important and inspirational people I've ever known. I'll never forget what she has done for me and her grandchildren. A very big shout-out to you, Mum. Your unwavering, motherly support is what I cherish the most – Thank you, and I love you!!

At the very same time, my in-laws, despite their own worlds being obliterated and rocked to the very core, have been there through everything, and they continue to show up for me and their grandchildren.

For this, I am eternally grateful and indebted to them both. Lyndon and I were extremely close to his parents, and as I mentioned earlier, I was worried about losing them. But the incident has brought us closer. A very big shout out to both my in-laws. I couldn't have made it this far without your continued support – Thank you and I love you more than you know!!

The gratitude that I have for those who have helped us is immense. Gratitude goes out to so many people, I truly can't list them all. However, the list does include my mum and parents-in-law as I've already mentioned, our close family friends, people from bowling (you know who you are), and my new family of affected people. I am grateful for each person reading my book, yes, you, too – Thank you for being you!

In late 2020, I had the absolute honour of meeting numerous people who had endured similar pain from losing a loved one to a workplace incident or who were themselves directly involved and injured in a workplace incident. To the two important ladies also affected by the incident, thank you both. I am grateful to have met all of them and to have been founding members with them of the NSW support group.

In that group, I worked very closely alongside my then co-chair, Matthew, and we formed a close bond. We'd always said we had each other's backs, and at the end of 2024, we tendered our resignations simultaneously. Matt and his wife, Teresa, have become much more than friends. They have become my family.

Their son, Luke, had a saying that he lived by - "Live fighting or die trying." He even went so far as to have it tattooed on his arm. Matt and Teresa lost Luke to a workplace incident and, subsequently, placed Luke's saying on his headstone and plaque at the fire station. They have been a voice and catalyst for change ever since.

Another inspirational person I've had the privilege of connecting with is the incredible Andrew Jobling via LinkedIn. Our initial interaction over a video call, where I shared my aspiration of writing a book, marked the beginning of a transformative journey at the end of

May, 2025. Andrew's unwavering support, encouragement, and expert guidance were instrumental in turning my book-writing dream from a mere idea into a tangible reality. His mentorship extended far beyond the realms of writing, shaping my path forward. Andrew's impact has been truly invaluable.

> *"Who knew I could possibly have such*
> *a profound impact on the lives of other people?"*
> – Andrew Jobling.

Well, Mr Jobling, I am yet another person you have had a profound impact on. You gave me the kick I needed to get this book finally out of my head and into the hands of many. Like you, I just want to have a positive impact on the lives of others.

One of my sessions with Andrew was about the WHY of book writing and it really got me thinking. He asked me hard-hitting questions from the get-go. He asked me what that voice inside my head was saying that would ultimately stop me from writing a book. It's really confronting when you have to actually put pen to paper and write those reasons down. My reasons were:

- I'm not good enough.
- I cannot write.
- Other people's opinions terrify me.
- I am easily distracted (I have ADHD after all)
- Who would want to publish my book; and
- The fear of recollecting events (reopening trauma).

When I read that, it almost felt like I was in a session with my psychologist. It was confronting, but I absolutely see why he got me to undertake this exercise. On the other hand, he said I want to know all the great characteristics and qualities about you. Again, another difficult one as I'm someone who doesn't like to talk about myself, and it was again, confronting at first, but with a bit of perseverance and with the help of Andrew, a list of qualities began to emerge. I got thinking:

- I am determined,
- I am being vulnerable,
- I am empathetic,
- I am dedicated,
- I am kind,
- I am gentle,
- I am honest and open,
- I am brave,
- I am extremely passionate,
- I am a change maker,
- I am creative,
- I am courageous,
- I am reliable,
- I am adaptable,
- I am resilient,
- I have a heart for others, and
- All with a desire to help others.

Andrew asked me if that is really how I see myself. Not even having to think about it, I replied with "absolutely." And that is the most powerful feeling looking back on that. WOW - I really do see all those qualities within myself. So now, whenever doubt creeps in, I can combat it with one of my qualities. Andrew, I will be forever grateful that you were able to show me this! From here on in, I know that I will succeed in becoming the author of my own successful story. And by sharing with the world and putting my vulnerability out there, I will be able to help other people. Even if it is only one person, I would be closer to reaching my goal of raising awareness.

Another inspirational moment came through my good friend, Patrizia Cassaniti, the lady I went on the "breakfast roadshow" with. Patrizia and her husband, Rob, have 3 children, one of whom is Christopher. Unfortunately, their son Christopher lost his life, just 4 days after his 18th birthday and one year after Lyndon's death, to a scaffold collapse in Sydney, NSW, Australia. Patrizia has used and continues to use her pain to deliver a message of workplace safety to everyone she meets.

Patrizia called and asked if I wanted to come down for the World premiere of the Pike River movie. Although I only had a few days' notice to plan, there was no way I was missing the opportunity. Pike River is a movie based on the true story of the 2010, NZ, Pike River mine disaster. The story shows how a friendship was formed between Anna (who lost her husband) and Sonya (who lost Ben, her youngest son), and Sonya's other son, who walked out of the mine, whilst also advocating for the 29 lives lost and fighting for real justice. As it is so close to what my mission is in life, it goes without saying I really wanted to see this and support the powerful initiative.

I travelled to Sydney from Brisbane in June 2025. This was a learning experience as we were welcomed into Patrizia's beautiful home and given the full show of a real Italian feast, and man, was it a beautiful feast. On the Saturday, we got to go to Christopher's memorial, and although I had driven under it a few times, I got to walk over the amazing Christopher Cassaniti Bridge. The feeling that overcame me was immense and so moving. Walking over this bridge dedicated to Christopher was surreal. Walking over it with his mother, Patrizia, was honouring. While at the same time, I felt we shouldn't have to have a bridge named after him, because he should still be here.

That evening, we travelled into the Sydney CBD to the State Theatre and watched the most moving movie that I have ever seen. I am probably biased because this movie hits so close to home as it was about workplace fatalities. But nonetheless, it was amazing. It was so captivating and so well played.

During bits and pieces, the audience would erupt into applause when the characters had their little wins. After the movie, they had the cast, producers and also the real Anna and Sonya up on stage for a Q&A session. Again, an amazing experience. My highlight from the premiere was personally meeting Anna, Sonya and Sonya's son, and explaining to them the impact the movie had as we too had experienced workplace deaths.

Another inspirational person is Dr Lana Cormie. We have built an incredible friendship now and often phone each other for either a general chit chat, assistance and moral support. Lana lost her husband, Charlie, in the Delacombe trench collapse in Victoria a few months before I lost Lyndon. We shared so many similarities from a multiple workplace fatality to how similar our men were. They were around the same age, we both had very young children, and they both were extremely hands-on fathers who would do absolutely anything for their families. Lana has always been an inspiration to me because she also has the fire in her belly to ensure that such needless killing does not happen to anyone. She was instrumental in the introduction of industrial manslaughter laws being introduced into Victoria. I am honoured to be able to call her my good friend.

A MOMENT OF REFLECTION

I truly believe that everybody comes into our lives for a purpose or a reason. That purpose or reason, we may never truly understand until much later in life; sometimes, we may never understand this.

I am lucky enough to know the reason for meeting most of the people I have. For me, the inspirational people I mentioned above have taught me so much about myself and life in general.

REFLECTION QUESTIONS:

1. Who is helping you? Who are you helping?
   When our incident occurred, I found myself scrolling the internet day in and day out, looking for answers. You see, when you are thrust into this realm, you have absolutely no help. Well, certainly back then we did not. Many of us are now pushing to help and assist other people going through what we have already faced. I found a few people who have proved to be a huge asset to me and my fight.

2. Can you have a long, hard think about people who have come into your life and think about what you have truly learned from them? This can be good or bad. Even people who come into your life who did not treat you the way you deserved, you can learn from. For example, if you had an abusive ex-partner, they may have taught you that you deserve so much better.

3. Who can you surround yourself with?
   I'm sure you have heard of the sayings such as "you are your surroundings."
   So, if the people you associate with bring you down, there is only one person that can change that narrative - YOU. Therefore, surround yourself with only positive people who lift you up, especially in times of need.

CHAPTER 15

PARENTING WHILST GRIEF STRICKEN

"Family is not an important thing. It's everything."

- MICHAEL J FOX

Michael J Fox has described it perfectly when it comes to family and it really hits home.

Shortly after the incident, I remember being brought to my knees when I was out shopping. I was casually strolling through the kids' clothing section of Myer when I looked up and a man caught my attention. He was clothes shopping with his little child. They were laughing and having a great old time. A regular day out, just creating those memories for them, I am sure. But for me, it was a real trigger and another simple, yet loud reminder of the obvious. A wave of despair washed over me and I lost it, uncontrollably bawling my eyes out. All because I knew I would never get to see Lyndon with his kids again, and the kids could never laugh with their daddy again.

Currently, as I write this, Chris is 17 and Mia is 16. When I think of that, it just doesn't seem real. It's really quite scary. I still remember the day they were both born. However, they were just 8 and 10 years old when their father was tragically killed. Lyndon was an extremely hands-on father. So they not only lost their father on that fateful day, but they also lost their best friend - as did I. The thoughts and feelings that run through your mind are indescribable when you are suddenly faced with having to tell your young children that daddy is never coming home and why. This is something I will NEVER forget. At those young ages, I knew they couldn't comprehend why or even how their lives had just been forever changed. The moment my husband died, I was quite literally thrust into the new world of solo parenting. An absolute battlefield to say the least. And to this day, it's not any easier and still different.

I had a few people compare me, a solo parent, to a single parent. Now, I may just get a few noses out of joint here, but I'm going to say it because few people don't notice the difference. That is a huge mistake! Single parents are single for a reason, normally by a choice of one or both parties. But their kids have a mother and a father who are still alive. Whereas solo parents are one parent trying to fill the void of the other, deceased parent. Every step you take, you are thinking about what they would do if they were still alive. Trying to guide your decisions that you are now required to make ALONE. It is bloody hard to say the very least! Please don't get me wrong, I'm not saying single parenting is easy (I know – my mum was a single mother), but I am writing from the separate and specific viewpoint of solo parenting with a deceased husband and father.

Someone said to Chris, who was 10 at the time of the incident, that he was now the man of the house. Whilst I understand that advice came from their heart and wasn't sinister, it's the absolute worst thing to say to a 10-year-old child. Because he took that literally. Chris lost a few years of his childhood when his dad died. And because of these events, he thought it was now his place to look after his mum and little sister. Such a thoughtful little man who just had his whole world upended. The next few years would see him not straying far from my side, especially when we had visitors over. He would often make an appearance and ask, "Are you OK, Mum?"

As Mia was just 8 years old at the time of her dad's death, apparently the processing in the brain differs. Mia doesn't talk much about losing her dad. However, she supports me in my quests when it comes to anything to do with her father and safety. The old saying says that everyone deals with grief differently. And Miss Mia is certainly no exception to this rule. Because she was slightly younger than her brother at the time she lost her father, she says she doesn't remember too much. That is also due to the trauma which, still to this day, gets pushed down further and further. It certainly scares me. Again, all of this could have simply been avoided!

Miss Mia has become such a little lady, and man oh man, can she draw! Her coping mechanisms have included, for quite a while now, reading a lot of books and drawing/sketching. And to be perfectly honest, if that's her way to deal with what she has had thrown at her, I'm all for it. I often say I don't know where she got that creative skill from, as it certainly wasn't me, hahaha.

I constantly try to talk about memories and there is one distinct memory which she told me recently. When Mia was about 6 or 7 years old, we had a neighbour move into the new estate where we lived. They had two boys who were about the same ages as Chris and Mia. Their youngest boy, a real blondie, got on exceptionally well with Mia. And for a while there, they were almost inseparable too. One day, when Lyndon and Mia were over at their house, Mia kissed this young lad - a dare and a only peck, I was told. And Lyndon's protective father mode was born – he grabbed Mia by the hand and took her straight home.

"Why would he do that, Mum?" she asked.

That moment was priceless. I was in complete hysterics, and I said, "Mia, that is one memory of Dad loving you that you never want to forget!"

Another conversation I remember was a rather in-depth discussion about employment and "adulting." I was explaining to her that you need to start at the bottom and work your way up. An analogy for many things in life. I continued by saying "My first job was at The Reject Shop, your auntie's was KFC and Dad, well, he was ... a milkman!"

The smile on her face said it all. Then she let out a little chuckle, "Wasn't that in the real old days?"

Again, I had to laugh. Don't they say, "Out of the mouth of babes?"

It's amazing, just to be able to give her snippets of information and facts about her dad. But bittersweet at the same time, as he should be here now, talking to her about these things, too.

I think Mia looks so much like Lyndon's mother and sister. But she is so funny with a dry sense of humour and is just like her dad in so many ways. She has recently enrolled into an Animal Care course to replace her schooling and it's honestly doing wonders for her.

Mia has now obtained her learner's driver's licence, which she is so excited about, already racking up almost half of her hours needed. We have just bought a new car for her, which was picked up in August 2025 – a cool Kia Cerato. In early 2025, Chris gained his provisional driver's licence, and true to our promise of buying the children their first cars, I purchased him a Mitsubishi Lancer. I now have two drivers in this house. How scary is that?

Chris has really taken to mucking about with whatever possible to make his car truly "his." He has made his car louder with the exhaust and spends as much time as he possibly can out in the shed "tinkering" with his car. One big thing about Lyndon was his passion for cars. As I said earlier in this book, Lyndon loved his Holdens. When Lyndon was 18, he would do exactly the same.

Master Chris (at the time of writing this, just shy of his 18th birthday) is a spitting image of his father, in absolutely every way possible. Approximately a month after his dad was killed, he said that he wanted to start ten-pin bowling. At first, I didn't want to face walking into the local bowling alley as so many of Lyndon's memories were in there. But it was a clear sign his son wanted to be as close as possible. A very good family friend of ours, Andrew, took him under his wing and began training him. Soon enough, Chris was on his way to becoming a true star, just like his dad.

Andrew had begun coaching Lyndon when he was just a few years older than Chris (about 13), and subsequently, they became teammates and, most of all, very good friends. Words cannot describe what it meant to me as Lyndon's wife and also to Lyndon's mum and dad, for Andrew to take on this mighty task. I will forever be indebted to Andrew for giving Chris this piece of his father. Chris has since gone on to bowl in some tournaments representing our home of Toowoomba and even South East Queensland.

To get into the QLD Team, he had to do his sporting resume, which was new to us. He put down his biggest goal - to win the annual Lyndon Quinlivan Graded Masters, a tournament created in honour of Lyndon, held in our hometown. I'm sure there was not a dry eye in the centre (from those that knew the significance) when, in 2023, Chrisso took home 1st place. He had reached his ultimate goal of winning his dad's tournament! We are just about to jet off to attend this event again for 2025, and, yes, of course he will be competing in this again.

Chris has since successfully gained a part-time, school-based apprenticeship with a local cabinet-making company and is doing very well on that front. He has just completed year 11 at his school, which is a trade college, hence the school-based apprenticeship. Now in 2026, he goes into year 12 to finish his education before going into the apprenticeship full-time. Chris absolutely loves his job and is learning daily, both at school and in his apprenticeship. However, unfortunately, he has already had 2 workplace incidents.

The latest injured his tendon in his left finger, requiring surgery. One of the hardest things as a parent is trying to teach your kids about employment when they are starting out and what their rights and responsibilities are within a workplace, especially having already gone through what we have. This naturally worried me, but I also know (OK, I am still learning) I cannot wrap him in cotton wool and he needs to learn just as all teenagers do. The positive thing to come out of this (remember, I try to look at everything with a positive attitude) is the way his workplace handled both situations. He is really lucky to have a great employer to begin his cabinetry career.

I promised both of my children that once they turned 16, they could get a tattoo in memory of their father. We obviously moved to sunny Queensland, and I recently found out that it's actually illegal in this state for under-18s. I was not letting that stop me from fulfilling my promise to my kids. So in December of 2024, Chris, my mother, and I travelled to NSW and Chris got his memory tattoo. I know a lot of people would never understand, but for me and Chris, it's god-damn perfect. And in December of 2025, again true to my promise, my mother, Mia and I went for a day trip to the same NSW tattooist to get Mia's memory tattoo. Mia picked it herself and all I can say is that we all love it.

A MOMENT OF REFLECTION

Our children are watching our example constantly. I had to walk a fine line because my way of dealing with the needless death of my husband was very different from my 2 young children's way of dealing with the sudden death of their father and best mate. Even then, their two ways are completely separate from each other because they are two individual people. One thing I knew for certain, I wanted the kids to see and watch me never giving up the fight for their father. They are okay with what I do, but even if they weren't, I'd hope that one day in the future, they would understand why I choose to fight.

REFLECTION QUESTIONS:

1. If one day you suddenly found yourself in a situation like mine, how do you think you would respond?

2. How do you cope when under immense pressure? Is it healthy? Everyone has a different coping strategy or mechanism. Some strategies could be seen as good whereas some can also be viewed as unhealthy. Do what is good and right for you.

2024, Chris' first tattoo at age 16. I absolutely love it and of course, so does he

2025, Mia's first tattoo at age 16. It suits her perfectly and is so petite

Chris aged 10. Dad will always be our hero

Chris and Mia in 2024, on our cruise to New Zealand

Chris and Al (his godfather) when Chris won his father's tournament in 2024. A very proud yet emotional day for us all

Mia's amazing drawing as a gift to me for Mothers Day, 2025

Chris bowling in his dad's tournament making us all very proud

From coaching the father at a young age to coaching the son.
Andrew and Chris

BOOK JACQUELINE AS A *SAFETY SPEAKER* TODAY

I had never envisaged that I would be a speaker, publicly sharing Lyndon's story to the world. Yet here I am. I vowed to Lyndon that I would never give up, never stop fighting for change, justice and accountability.

That change can never happen for us and I have accepted that, for the most part. However, I chose to share this story knowing that it WILL make a difference in somebody else's life. Another business will hear the message to ensure that their employees go home to their loved ones at the end of their shift.

I present my true and raw lived experience to companies both big and small, Australia-wide as well as online. I have spoken at large safety conferences, in schools where the next generation of our workforce is coming from, small to medium sized businesses, regional roadshows, and large training and safety organisations. I can come to your worksite or visit via an online video platform.

If you would like to book me personally to come and speak at one of your events, please get in touch by contacting me one of the following ways:

Phone: (Australia +61) 0403 017 530

Email: admin@jacquelinequinlivan.com.au

Website: www.jacquelinequinlivan.com.au

Jacci speaking on stage at the Brisbane Work Health & Safety show, March, 2026

Jacci speaking on stage at the NSCA Conference, March, 2026

Jacci, March, 2026

IMPORTANT CONTACTS

I have created a list of the following contacts who have been mentioned in my book, or whom I simply think would be of use. I'd really love to hear from you if sharing my story changed your mindset on safety within your workplace, if you have suffered adversity and chosen to rise above, or simply if you want to know more.

- **Patrizia Cassaniti**
  www.touchedbychristopher.org.au
  www.letstalkaboutsafety.com.au - There is the ability to donate here to support the families who find themselves faced with a workplace fatality.

- **Andrew Jobling**
  The amazing man behind pushing me to get my book out into the world.
  www.andrewjobling.com.au
  Ph: +61 414 973 315

- **Safe Work Australia**
  www.safeworkaustralia.gov.au

- **First Light Widowed Association**
  https://www.firstlight.org.au/

- **Camp magic**
  For kids 7 to 17 who have lost a parent, sibling or guardian.
  https://www.feelthemagic.org.au
  Ph: 1300 602 465

- **Wombats Wish**
  For kids 5 to 17 who have lost a parent/carer.
  https://www.wombatswish.org.au
  Ph: (03) 9069 0314 or +614 9996 6228

- **Beyond Blue**
  www.beyondblue.org.au
  Ph: 1300 224 636

- **Lifeline**
  www.lifeline.org.au
  Ph: 13 11 14

- **Mates in Construction**
  www.mates.org.au
  Phone: 1300 642 111

- **This is a Conversation Starter (TIACS)**
  Mental Health Counselling.
  www.tiacs.org
  Call/text 0488 846 988 (in Australia)

- **Morpheus Publishing**
  Morpheus Publishing and Justine, my amazing publisher, made this a tangible product possible. A huge shoutout goes to these guys. If you've ever wanted to write your own book, I highly recommend getting in touch.

  www.morpheuspublishing.com.au
  hello@morpheuspublishing.com.au
  +61403564942

REFERENCES

Work-related fatalities, *Safe Work Australia.* Available at: https://data.safeworkaustralia.gov.au/interactive-data/topic/work-related-fatalities (Accessed: 30.03.2026)

New estimates on the costs of raising children in Australia, 17.04.2018. *Australian Institute of Family Studies.* Available at: https://aifs.gov.au/media/new-estimates-costs-raising-children-australia

Confined Spaces, *Safe Work, NSW.* Available at: https://www.safework.nsw.gov.au/hazards-a-z/confined-spaces (Accessed: 30.03.2026)

SafeWork NSW v Norske Skog Paper Mills, *Caselaw, NSW*. Available at: https://www.caselaw.nsw.gov.au/decision/174be35ee49dc41d188b23cd

Workers Compensation, *State Insurance Regulatory Authority, NSW*. Available at: https://www.sira.nsw.gov.au/workers-compensation

Compensation Claims Guide, *State Insurance Regulatory Authority, NSW*. Available at: https://www.sira.nsw.gov.au/workers-compensation-claims-guide/understanding-the-claims-journey/other-compensation-payable

www.ingramcontent.com/pod-product-compliance
Lightning Source LLC
LaVergne TN
LVHW020046110826
845155LV00029B/645